Running Mascara

Embracing the Beauty of an Imperfect Church

Tiffany Wasson

BOOK DEDICATION:

I would like to dedicate this book to my husband, Jeremy. I will never forget when we first met and will always remember our first serious conversations. I told you that I was a mess and came with a lot of baggage. Despite the amount I shared, you told me, "It's your imperfections that make you beautiful."

Throughout our years of marriage, you have continued to love me for me with the love of Christ, looking past my imperfections. Thank you for your endless hours of listening to me during my struggles, encouraging me, and always pointing me to Jesus. You are the love of my life, my best friend, and truly a gift from God. I am so thrilled to be sharing this amazing journey called life with you.

TABLE OF CONTENTS

ACKNOWLEDGMENTS

$\mathscr{I}$ am overwhelmed at the number of people who have helped me and have believed in me throughout this process. Honestly, thank you just doesn't seem to cut it…All of you will never know the depth of my gratitude. "I thank my God ever time I remember you" (Philippians 1:3).

To Donald Newman at Xulon Press, when I met you at the 2015 Velocity Conference, I was immediately inspired. Through your continual encouragement and prayers, not only have I finished my first book, but I have also been set free from so many strongholds.

To the rest of my Xulon Press team, for going above and beyond the call of duty to help get my message out there. Even more than that, you helped me dream again.

To Dr. Larry Keefauver, for taking the time to read my manuscript and offer suggestions. You opened up my eyes and helped me to see my book in a different light. My book is better because of you.

To my sister Kristen Campbell, you created the amazing book cover for Running Mascara. You made me look better than I really do and created exactly what I envisioned for the front cover! You are so talented sis! You rock!

To Elizabeth Gay, for not only being an amazing sister in Christ but for the willingness to always double-check my work. I would be lost without you girl!

To Mary and Caleb Riggins, for sharing a huge part of your life with me to be placed in the middle of these pages. Without your story the book would not be complete.

To my husband Jeremy and my sons Aaron and Austin, for encouraging me daily to write this book! You believed in me even when I didn't believe in myself.

To all of my family and friends, thank you for sticking by me through all of my hardships in my life. No matter how dark it got—all of you at different times were lights that brought me home time and time again.

To Paul and Vickie Hafer and the rest of the Lighthouse Christian Broadcasting family in Saint Marys, Georgia. I would not be the woman I am today if it wasn't for all of you. I am eternally grateful for each of you. No matter where I am in life, you are always in my heart.

To Greenbrier Church, for being a rock for our family to lean on. The Lord put all of you in our lives at the right time and our family is better for it!

To Jeremy Ownby, for filming my Kickstarter video and really bringing my project to life. You always go out of your way to serve anyone you can. Trust me when I say — it doesn't go unnoticed! Your hard work is so appreciated.

To everyone who so humbly gave financially towards this project I am blown away at your generosity. Todd Williams and Steve Brown, you truly out did yourselves.

To the people who committed to pray for me throughout this process, you have no idea how many roadblocks you prayed me through!

And to God…You are my everything and I am nothing without You!

The sacrifice pleasing to God is a broken spirit.
God, You will not despise a broken and humble heart.

~Psalm 51:17

Running Mascara

Perfect makeup, a mask upon your face
To hide the pain inside; longing to embrace
Something that is real, true, and can set you free,
But too afraid to embrace the true reality.

Perfect hair that falls in place and never out of line,
To hide the sin from coming out.
Hoping and praying that no one sees inside,
The one who is truly broken and needs a Savior to revive.

Perfect life that always seems to walk a straight path
To hide the falls that come, longing to steer away others' wrath.
Everyone thinks that a superhero resides with the way that
you shine,
But they miss all of the times when you wish that you
could hide.

Hide your face from the world so that the mask can be gone,
Where freedom finally comes and you can change the tide.
Look! No one is watching; you can finally step out of line!
There is freedom around the corner when facing your
imperfect side.

Running mascara, there is beauty here-it's called the "ugly cry,"

When you let it all out and truly embrace who you are inside.

You are shattered glass and no longer need to hide

The fact that you are broken and need a Savior to thrive.

~Tiffany Wasson

Introduction:

A LETTER TO THE CHURCH

My heart raced wildly as I spun in circles round and round, watching the world pass me by. I could feel the blood in my veins creeping slowly from the center of my body into the tips of my fingers. My head felt like a hot air balloon firing off into the sky. Unable to stand any longer, I collapsed as my legs gave way beneath me.

As I lay flat on my back, the smell of freshly cut grass raced into my nose like waves crashing onto the shore, taking over every other smell. Finally, after my head had stopped spinning, I was able to make out the shape of every cloud in the sky above me. "How can life get any better than this?" I thought to myself as ladybugs marched their way onto my skin.

I loved the outdoors, which was kind of strange, considering I was a seven-year-old girl. There were not many girls my age who liked to be outside in the dirt and filth.

My hair fell to my shoulders and was white as snow — at least, when I cleaned it. To the naked eye, it was dirty-blonde from playing everything from hide-and-seek to basketball, from baseball to wallball. My clothes were always stained or ripped from sliding into first base or falling off my bike.

Sure, my parents bought me nice clothes, but I refused to wear them. I wore my tears like a trophy because they represented all my scars and previous adventures. I was a loogie-spitting, rough-playing, dirt-swimming tomboy. When you grow up with three older brothers, it is almost impossible to become anything less. One of my favorite places to be was in their shadows, chasing them and imitating their every move. I was a wild, free-spirited, daddy's little girl, with a fire that burned deep inside with the love of the Lord. I felt as if I could conquer the world; nothing could ever stop me — nothing.

At least, that is what I believed. Through one dreaded phone call between my parents, everything in my life change, and my perfect world was shaken. I started to face situations that I never dreamed I would have to face, and to my surprise, I faced most of them alone. I was too afraid to speak up, and that does something awful to a person. In the course of my struggles, something began to happen, and my mind-set started to change. The little girl who loved the gaps in her teeth, her big ears, and torn clothes started to pick apart how different she really was, as if it were a bad thing.

I started noticing other girls around me who dressed differently than I did, who did not play outside as much, and who cared more about dating boys than playing in the dirt with them. Furthermore, as my scope in life expanded, my attention was zoned in on girls on the covers of magazines — makeup so perfectly fashioned, hair in place, and clothes that stayed intact without holes or stains. Was I supposed to remain the free-spirited person I had started out in life to be, or was I supposed to be more like the girls in the magazines? I wanted to fit in as much as possible, so I started to make changes in order to mirror their image.

I wish I could say that self-image is where my addiction stopped, but eventually the desire to look the part started to invade my mental and spiritual life as well. Little by little, the world began to peel back the layers of who I really was and started to change me from the inside out, and not in a good way. Believe it or not, most of these changes took place when I found myself at Texas Bible Institute right out of high school. Texas Bible Institute has a nine-month go-to-grow program that is not accredited for college credit, but it gave me the opportunity to have nine months of my life drenched with the Lord with out any distractions. Initially, I went to work on my gifts for the Lord, but in the process, things did not go as planned and got pretty nasty.

I had the "pleasure" of rooming with seven other females (four bunk beds, one closet, and one bathroom — a nightmare waiting to happen). Faced with all these "perfect" girls on a daily basis and fed spiritually by some of the greatest Christian speakers in the country, I started to question, not only if I looked right, but also if I was doing *anything* right. Slowly I lost my passion for the Lord, and I desired to be flawless in body, mind, and spirit. In order to obtain the unattainable, I pushed myself harder than I ever had in my entire life.

Sadly, I traveled this self-destructive path more than once during my young adult life until one day I hit a brick wall. In that moment, I realized that I was tired, worn, and leaving absolutely no room for Jesus. I had fooled myself into thinking I could handle everything on my own without Him, and that I could clean myself up and stay clean. The free-spirited girl who had started out with a fire in her belly and a love for the Lord began to be extinguished. I was trying so hard to shove myself into a "perfect Christian" mold that I was literally starving my body, mind, and spirit of what they really needed—more food and Jesus. I was not able to embrace my imperfections, my brokenness, and my constant need for a Savior because I was too busy trying to fix myself.

Now, with all that being said, I have some questions to ask you, the church, as the bride of Christ...

1. *Do you often compare yourself and your life to those around you?*
2. *Do you feel like you fail at everything?*
3. *Do you have an all or nothing type of personality?*

4. *Do you seem to hide the way you are truly feeling by putting on a happy face?*

5. *Do you avoid talking about your personal life or have trouble letting others in?*

6. *Do you fail to ask for prayer from others when you need it the most?*

7. *Do you pile on as many tasks as you can at church or at home to make yourself feel better?*

8. *Do you feel guilt instead of conviction when you miss prayer time, bible reading, or church?*

9. *Do you avoid saying hello to new people that come to church or fail to ask new people to come to church, because they do not fit into the "mold" of so called "church goers"?*

10. *Do you feel like you have to clean yourself up before God accepts you?*

If you answered, "yes" to four out of ten of these questions then you are in danger of striving for perfection in your life, leaving no room for Jesus. You may be at risk of trying to fit into a particular mold instead of spinning wildly and uncontrollably, embracing your imperfections so that your constant need for a Savior is embraced. Instead of fooling ourselves, like I did, we need to wear our brokenness as a crown. We need to let others know that it is okay to not have everything together or figured out, because we will never "arrive" until we get to heaven.

If we are not careful, perfectionism can invade our personal lives and, more dangerously, the church. Not only does the striving for perfection cause us to starve the body of Christ of what it really needs — more of Jesus — but it also makes it impossible for new members to become a part of the family of God. New members are turned away by their inability to measure up. People start to wonder, "Am I doing any of this right?"

My prayer is that we Christians would tear off the need to be flawless before the world around us. We need to learn to wear our brokenness proudly in order to be closer to our Savior and reach more people for Him. Jesus wants us to be in a place of constant desperation for Him to be our strength and our identity, and for Him to be everything for our eternity. True freedom comes from realizing how broken we really are and embracing that in the loving arms of the Savior.

He is waiting on you, Christian. He is waiting on you, church. Are you ready for freedom?

Part 1

SHATTERED

*It's what's buried deep inside that frightens me
because it's broken, like a shattered mirror.*
~ Jessica Sorensen
The Secret of Ella and Micha

My heart shattered, my world shattered.
~Richelle Mead
Shadow Kiss

CHAPTER 1: MY HAPPY PLACE

Just think of happy thoughts and you'll fly.

~Walt Disney

Peter Pan

The smell of paint filled the autumn air as the door remained under lock and key. The suspense was killing me. I could not wait to find out what my dad was doing behind closed doors. I thought none of us kids knew what was going on, but with all of the muttering under breath and the knowing glances from my brothers and my mom, it seemed that everyone except me knew. The fact that everyone knew about it and I didn't made me extremely angry, like a volcano ready to erupt.

See, it wasn't just a typical "decorating the room" day. There was a lot at stake. My oldest brother, Tim, had moved out a little while before in preparation for college, dating, and marriage, which meant that the two bedrooms dedicated to children were up for a major shift—I hoped that one of them would be *all* mine. I mean, I was the only girl out of four children, so I thought, "Of course I will have my own room. I am the only girl." However, Charles was the oldest child left in the house, so the odds were not in my favor.

I had been sharing a room with the youngest of my three brothers, Joseph, since I was born, which wasn't terrible because he did bring me great comfort. Naturally, being the youngest and the only girl surrounded by protection, I was the scaredy cat of the family. Although I liked the aspect of having a hero on call during thunderstorms and strange noises outside the window, I was not a fan of having the head of my favorite Cabbage Patch doll repeatedly thrown against our orange bunk bed.

Honestly, the abuse to my doll was extremely exaggerated. I called him Danny, and he had so many battle scars across his face that he looked like an Oompa-Loompa. My brother would relentlessly give my doll a meeting with the bunk bed while I screamed in the background. I wasn't quite sure if the violent behavior against my buddy would stop if I had my own room, but I could only hope.

The curious thoughts danced long enough in my brain, and I just couldn't take it anymore—I had to know what was going on in the forbidden room. Since no one would spill their guts, I decided to take matters into my own hands and figure out the truth against all odds. While everyone was talking in the kitchen, I slowly snuck out the front door, tiptoeing as if broken glass were all over the ground. I even made sure that the screen door wouldn't slam and give way

to my location. I helped it close quietly and continued with
my devious yet intelligent plan.

I dropped quickly to the ground like a Navy SEAL on a
black-op mission. I crawled on my belly through the dirt and
the filth, welcoming the mess I was creating on my clothes
once again. I crawled all the way through the back of the
bushes, causing new snags on my shirt to mark proof of a
new adventure. I shrugged off the bugs that hit my face and
the gnats that made their way into my mouth. I was on a
mission, and nothing could stop me.

Finally, I reached my destination, and I slowly rose, little
by little, until I was eye level with the front two windows of
our house. As the smell of paint filled my sinuses, I saw it—
pink. The vibrant pink walls shined beautifully before me. I
rubbed my eyes with my filthy hands to look one more time
to make sure that I wasn't dreaming.

"Tiffany—no! What are you doing?" my brother Joseph
screamed at a distance. He sounded as if he were my personal drill sergeant yelling in my ear to get me to keep doing
push-ups.

I ducked down past the bushes as if I could still conceal
my location at that point in time. My brother pulled me out
against my will as I threw my body around to try to get
loose and break free. I was caught dirty-handed—literally.
He continued, "Mom and Dad were trying to surprise you
about *your* new room!"

27

I couldn't believe my ears and my eyes. I knew I had seen the pink, but I still could not wrap my mind around the idea of *my room,* and in one of the most glorious colors on the planet — pink — my favorite color of all time. I was at a loss for words. I almost couldn't move but since I had spoiled the surprise, they let me walk into the room instead of waiting any longer.

Shock and Awe

When I stepped into *my* new room, I was in girl heaven. I was going to have my own room, away from boys, orange bunk beds, and stinky feet. I even got my grandmother's old vanity. Now, I was ecstatic about the pink room but I was more excited about the vanity. I loved the dome-shaped mirror, the side drawers that smelled of cedar, the beautiful bench that sat in front, and the secret drawer underneath where I could hide all my treasures, especially my tooth fairy money, from the rest of the household.

I rubbed my fingers across the newly placed piece of furniture and sat down at the vanity in awe, full of happiness and feeling loved by my family. I could not believe that they would go through all that trouble to surprise me, the baby girl of the family. Life was great, and I was in my happy place. I was able to be both a tomboy and a girl who loved pink all at the same time, and it was not a big deal with the world, or at least not in our little household.

The Perfect Balance

Most of the time I was welcomed as one of the guys by resting in my brothers' shadows. They longed, not only to protect me whenever they could, but also to teach me all their tricks. I learned from the best on how to play manhunt without getting caught, wallball without getting out, and how to slide into second base with out breaking a leg.

I was even taught how to punch someone in the face if someone tried to hurt me. I am not kidding at all. Charles, my middle brother, would get on his knees, eye level with me, and shout in my face, "Tiffany, punch me!" For the life of me, I could never bring myself to punch him as hard as he wanted me to, because he was my brother and I loved him. But at least I was prepared on the "how to" of knocking someone out with my "lethal hands" if necessary.

Aside from mimicking boy times with my brothers, I also had my girl times with my two best friends in the neighborhood. Because of my newly decorated room, we were able to have freedom from boys, if we so desired. We could finally come over to my house without being bombarded with, well, all things boy. In addition, we rode our pink bikes around the neighborhood, cruised in our matching white-and-pink skates, hiked the backwoods of our neighborhood as we sang along to New Kids on the Block and the *Lion King* soundtrack, and so much more. Then, at the end of the day, I was the only girl in a family full of boys, and I was fully loved.

As long as I could, I lived my life in perfect balance between girlie happiness with my two best friends and amazing adventures with my brothers. I was oblivious to anything else going on in the world around me. To me, everyone seemed just as happy as ever. I had no idea that the perfect picture frame of the life that I was in was about to be dropped onto the hard floor beneath my feet as the glass within shattered to the point of no return.

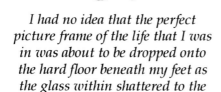

I had no idea that the perfect picture frame of the life that I was in was about to be dropped onto the hard floor beneath my feet as the glass within shattered to the point of no return.

On an unforgettable summer day, I would learn the cold, hard truth that everything in my life wasn't flawless. I had been living in a land of make-believe. Unfortunately, throughout my life, I have been unsuccessful in forgetting that day. The memory has been forever ingrained in my mind and in my heart, and it can never be erased.

Reflection:

Can you remember a period or certain periods in your life where everything seemed to be perfect? Can you recall good things and bad things about these particular moments?

Scripture Focus:

Psalm 34: 8, "Taste and see that the LORD is good. How happy is the man who takes refuge in Him!"

CHAPTER 2: THE DREADED CALL

If God brings you to it…He will see you through it.

~Timothy Pina

Hearts for Haiti: Book of Poetry & Inspiration

I charged inside for a break from the hot sun beating down on my skin on a late, musty July afternoon. In southern Georgia during the summer, the sun is an unforgiving brutal source of energy refusing to give way. I wanted a popsicle, my favorite summer treat, to bring some relief to my dry palate. I ran around the corner as if I were racing against time, trying to get back outside before anyone noticed me.

To my surprise, the phone demanded attention. "Ring, ring, ring," the telephone sounded.

"I'll get it," I shouted as I dashed around the hallway corner towards the phone to answer its call.

"Hello." I was too late, because my dad's voice beat mine. He continued, "Honey, is that you?"

"Yes, John, it's me, your wife. We need to talk," my mom thundered.

"What is wrong with you, Laura?" my dad said as his voice cracked with fear and trembled, as if he had known this moment was coming and wished that it could be deleted from his existence.

My mom's voiced cracked in the beginning as if tears were trying to break through. In order to keep them from coming, she quickly thundered back before she hung up the phone. "John, you know what is wrong and what we have to do to fix it. There is just no other way. The lawyer wants to meet with us both tomorrow, so be as ready as you can be." She hung up and the phone beeped, giving further proof that her presence was no longer on the other side.

Lawyer? Fix it? What were they talking about? Why did my mom sound so angry? I had never heard her speak to my dad in that tone before, while trying to hold back so much sadness. I had never heard so much fear and trembling in my dad's voice either; his voice had always been so stern and full of confidence. I could not comprehend what was going on. My nine-year-old self tried to hold back the tears, but they came rushing into my eyes uncontrollably, like a river bursting through a dam too weak to keep the water from crashing through. I used my shirt to quickly wipe away the tears before anyone could see the pain written all over my face.

"Don't worry, Tiffany. Everything is okay; your parents are happy. It's only a nightmare—wake up! Everything is okay—*everything is okay!*" I recited to myself over and over as I walked away in denial. I made my way outside to play so that I could throw what I had just heard into a pit of distractions and bury the pain with a new adventure. Sadly, I was able to do that for only a short period of time, because before I could even catch my next breath, it seemed the sun was trying to lay its head to rest and I got the dreaded call from the house.

"Tiffany, it is time to come inside. It's getting dark," my mom shouted from the porch.

"But Mom, Sarah, Karen, and I wanted to ride our bikes to our favorite spot. Can't I come in when we're done?" I pleaded, as if I were going to die if she said no. I kind of knew the pain that was to follow, and I was not ready to face it. I just wanted to run away.

"Tiffany Anna Marie Williams!" she shouted, in the tone that all kids learn from their parents, the tone that says if they do not obey, something fierce is going to happen. It's the type of tone that shakes the earth below and then rumbles throughout the entire body. Then it slowly takes the next breath away. Yep, that is the one. I hated when she used that voice and all four of my names. But even more, I hated going inside. Reluctantly obeying my mom's call, I grabbed my bike and went inside, not ready to face my fate.

Gut Wrenching

"Tiffany, come into the kitchen. We need to talk," my mom said with hesitation as soon as I came in. Was I in trouble? For the first time in my life, I hoped to God that I was. I slowly edged my way into the kitchen, worried sick about what was to come.

I turned the corner and saw my dad. His face was blood-shot-red from tears that had been pouring from his eyes. My heart dropped to my stomach, and my knees felt weak. I had never seen my dad cry before; it was the most horrendous sight I had ever seen. My mom had tears starting to build up in her eyes too. She finally broke the silence and spoke the awful words: "Kids, your father and I are getting a divorce."

And there it was. I fell to the ground and wept hysterically. I could not believe what my ears were hearing and what I was feeling in my heart. My dad, full of compassion, swept me up with his rough but gentle hands and wrapped his loving arms around me. I loved his arms. In his arms, there were no worries and no fear. My three brothers tried to stay strong for me, but even they could not bury the feelings that were conquering them deep inside.

I could not comprehend why the big "D" was happening to my parents. Divorce happened only to my friends' parents who were not happy. My parents were happy and had never seemed to have any problems. But the more I thought about it, the more things made sense; the puzzle pieces finally came together. Whenever I had seen my dad sleeping on the couch, it was not because he snored. It was because my parents' love for each other had been melting away.

I was infuriated; I felt sick. I felt as if I had just run a marathon in hundred-degree weather, gasping for air and trying to get one more breath before my chest collapsed. My perfect life had

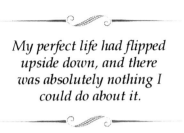

My perfect life had flipped upside down, and there was absolutely nothing I could do about it.

flipped upside down, and there was absolutely nothing I could do about it.

Big Changes

I had not blinked an eye before my world began to change, and like a mediocre kayaker attempting to paddle in a class-four rapid, it was hard to keep afloat. My dad, whom I loved very much, my knight in shining armor, had to leave my side and move out. To make matters worse, my middle brother Charles left with my dad so that he wouldn't have to live alone. I had already had one of my brothers move out, and now another one had to go. Sure, I had my pink room, but I would have given all that away for my family to be back together again.

My dad and my brother Charles only moved about ten miles from the house but they moved into a trailer that could hardly be defined as a home. I felt so bad for them. The outside was a rusty-orange color, and the inside smelled like an old grandma who smoked cigars and tried to cover it up with cheap perfume.

I missed the men in my life so much it hurt. My two oldest brothers were off doing their own thing most of the time. My youngest brother, Joseph, didn't spend much time with me because I was not his age and was not cool enough. Plus, he was dealing with all of the changes in his own way. Needless to say, that left me alone a lot of the time.

When it came to my dad, although I did not get to stay with him every day, my mom did make sure that I got to see him. I saw him probably every other weekend, and sometimes during the week, which still wasn't enough for me. I was use to having him around all of the time. However, I realized that I could not control the situation and had to take what I was given, even if I felt like they were table scraps. And although his trailer wasn't "home," whenever I could visit my dad, we made the most of it. I loved being with him.

As time went on, against my siblings' will and my will, both our parents found new love. My mom brought a new man into our lives. His name was Mark. He stood five feet ten inches, his hair was as dark as the night, and his skin had the same tone as a Cherokee Indian's. His eyes had a hint of green, and whenever they gazed into my mine, they burned inside my soul. He was really funny, a great cook, and seemed to really like us kids. But I had the hardest time completely accepting him because I missed the one I thought he was taking the place of.

My dad found new love too. Her name was Marie, just like my middle name. She was a schoolteacher, and boy, you could tell, because she had enough patience for us kids to go around. She had beautiful brown hair and hazel eyes. Her hands were gentle and always found time for helping us kids. Her presence brought so much comfort, and she always had a way to make me smile. Oftentimes I would hold back the laughs because I felt guilty for being happy.

Was I allowed to be happy when my family was so shattered? I was confused. The whole new world I was living in was uncharted territory. Now, I understood what Christopher Columbus must have felt like on his first attempt to reach America—confused, frightened, and unprepared. I was being led blindly, and I didn't know where life was taking me.

Of course, my parents' new loves did not bring just two new people into our lives, but five more girls. Mark had three daughters, and Marie had two daughters. The change was huge for me. I was no longer the only girl. I had to share the attention I got from my family with *five* other girls.

Mark would bring his girls around, and they started to invade my inner circle by playing with my friends and me. Marie's girls were much older and I though it was nice to have some older sisters, but I wasn't ready for any of that at all. There were too many changes, too fast. All of the sudden, I had to share everything: my mom, my dad, my brothers, my adventurous bike, and my friends. My whole world was invaded, including my personal space.

Discipline

I remember the first time that my stepdad, Mark, spanked me. His daughters and I were playing in the front yard, and an argument of some sort broke out. I do not recall what it was about, but I remember all too well the aftermath. Once the situation escalated, we all got called to the backyard. We all slowly came around the fence, and Mark spanked us. I was so upset. I understood discipline because my parents disciplined me all of the time, and honestly, the spanking wasn't even that bad. I just wasn't ready to accept it from someone so new to my life.

Even more than that, I did not take it very well when my own parents disciplined me. Most of the time, the only thing my mom had to do was to say my full name and I would cry. I hated being in trouble and disappointing others. So needless to say, when someone other than my mom or dad spanked me at that particular moment in my life, I burned with anger.

The moment that Mark's hand made contact with my bottom, I wanted my daddy more than ever. I wanted my life back. I didn't want to share everything that I had with his daughters. I didn't want to compete with Marie's daughters for attention. I had so much emotional whiplash that I was exhausted, completely wrung out of all my strength. Furthermore, from what I could remember, my dad had never spanked me.

My dad carried with him a huge belt around his waist. He was a lineman for Georgia Power, and his belt wasn't one of those fake leather ones. It was pure leather and about half an inch thick. His belt had been a gift from his dad; it had been his grandfather's, who had used it in his barbershop as his sharpening strap. It was so thick that you could hear it as it cranked past each belt loop when he took it out to use it.

The child in danger of getting a spanking would feel as if they were being cranked to the top of a roller coaster and about to have the worst ride of their life. He would use it to spank all of us kids—well, at least most of us. I am not saying I never did anything wrong, but my dad could not bring himself to spank me, his baby girl.

I can recall the one time that he attempted to spank me. He took me into the bathroom to leave a mark with his belt. Tears filled my eyes, and I was not ready for the pain that I was going to have to endure. He cranked that belt out of each belt loop—*crank, crank, crank, crank*—and he doubled that thing over to snap it.

The sound of the snap was awful, and every hair on my body stood at attention. Then he looked at me, and tears finally filled his eyes. He leaned down to eye level with me and whispered, "Tiffany, start crying. Leave the bathroom crying so that everyone will think that you got a spankin'."

I loved my dad for that moment. He did his best to protect me from pain. I did get my fair share of quick smacks on the bottom or a few catches on the leg with a flyswatter. But he could not use that gigantic belt on his little, scrawny daughter. I was thankful for his mercy.

A New World, A New Me

All these signs point to the fact that Mark and Marie did not immediately bring joy into our lives, and neither did their kids. But my brothers and I could tell that both of our parents were happier because of it, and that was a hard thing to accept. How were we, my brothers and I, supposed to take all this change, this new life? Our family was no longer a unified puzzle. We were scattered all over the ground as if a person had given up and out of frustration decided to toss all the pieces onto the floor because they were unable to figure out how they fit back together.

And luck would have it, just when I thought nothing else could be altered in my life; I received further news from my mom. She sat me down to let me know that she had decided she wanted to move to St. Simons Island, Georgia. She told me of its beauty and how much fun I would have, but it was so hard to listen to every single word coming out of her mouth. All I was thinking about was those I would be leaving behind. "It is only three hours away, Tiffany. And I promise that you will be able to see your dad and your brothers as often as you want to," she said confidently. Then she continued, "What do you say, sweet girl?"

"Okay, Mom, as long as you promise I can see Dad as much as possible," I said with a hint of uncertainty and with my head hanging low. I knew that seeing him every day was not going to be a possibility and would be totally out of reach. But what else was I supposed to say? My mom sounded really excited about the move, and I wanted her to be happy. So without further hesitation, my mom, Mark, my brother Joseph, and I moved to St. Simons Island, leaving behind my dad and my brothers Tim and Charles. My life had fallen apart, split in two, all before my tenth birthday, and slowly but surely I began to change on the inside.

As things changed, I began to be a little more introverted and not as willing to face each day with confidence, lacking the fearlessness I once had possessed. However, through my pain, I started to notice others around me. It didn't matter if I was on a school bus, at a park, or sitting in my living room with others; I started to wonder the kind of pain they were in. I would constantly look at people on my left, right, front, and back. If there was no one around me, I would often think of others. I would take a mental picture and wonder how their lives were. Had they just gone through a divorce? Had they just lost a family member? I was overtaken by compassion.

I started to realize that everyone carries with them a book, a story written long before I would see them in the chapter I became a part of. God revealed to me that not all stories were fairy tales; everybody had a story that they tried to shove into their back pocket and hide from the rest of the world. I learned that people often seemed like they had it all together, but most of the time, that was not the case. I understood that not every story had a tragic chapter, but every single person who ended up in front of me did have something that had come into their lives and shaped them to become the person they were.

I also knew that when I tried to portray a perfect person without a past, I wasn't helping anyone around me; and I could tell that people wanted to break free from the cage around them but didn't know how. Contrary to my desire to be all to myself, I would ask others how they were doing. Instead of doing like most people and asking "How are you today?" without really caring how a person was, I would wait for a deeper answer than just "Fine." People would not usually share much because they seemed too embarrassed to share, it was just too painful to share, or no one had ever tried to listen to them before. However, I had a heart for others and ears that wanted to listen.

But my listening was short-lived. I was in too much pain to care about others and their problems or to let others in. I would hear the surface stories that people put forth to make it look like they were perfectly in line, and I would choose to dig no further. I had my own problems to worry about. Truth be told, it became easier to glance at people's faces, see the surface, and be fine with whatever they handed to me, because I wanted them to accept my mask as well.

Deep down inside, I wanted to live out Galatians 6:2, which challenges us to "carry each other's burdens, and in this way you will fulfill the law of Christ." I longed to hear people's stories and help them feel a weight lifted. I wanted to set others free from their bondage by helping them. But honestly, I was the one who needed chains removed. Unfortunately, freedom was far off because the pain of my parents' divorce was just the beginning of my captivity. When my mom decided to move us, I started to face a lot of opposition in my new school in a way that I had never thought I would.

Reflection:

Has there been a time in your life when everything fell apart? Did it make you calloused to everything and everyone around you? How did this moment or moments change you overall as a person?

Scripture Focus:

Deuteronomy 31: 8, "The LORD is the one who will go before you. He will be with you; He will not leave you or forsake you. Do not be afraid or discouraged."

Galatians 6:2, "Carry one another's burdens; in this way you will fulfill the law of Christ."

CHAPTER 3: MEAN GIRLS

You may be pretty, and you may be talented, but nobody will remember that if you're mean.

~Katie Holmes

When I say that I had gaps in my teeth as a little girl, I am not exaggerating one bit. I had *big* gaps. The biggest one I had was right in the center of my mouth, between my top two front teeth. I could put a large Tootsie Pop stick between those puppies with out a fight. I actually loved to do that as a little girl; it was one of my favorite tricks.

My three older brothers would make fun of me all the time for my gaps. My brother Charles, the funny one, would say as he threw his hands into the air, "Smile, Tiffany. Man, I don't know if I should smile back at you or kick a field goal." Sometimes my brothers would even call me "hockey puck" because they said that the gap was big enough to fit one through.

In the beginning, it would sting when they said those things, but eventually I was able to laugh at myself. I mean, they were my brothers, and that is what siblings do. Besides, we all kind of picked on one another for different things, and truthfully, it didn't matter what they said as long as they let me follow them around.

I loved them and they loved me, and to top it off, they were my heroes. But something began to happen on the inside of me, when people outside my family safety circle started to make fun of me. That kind of experience hurts pretty deep, and it takes a long time to dig the pain out. It's like an annoying splinter in a hard-to-reach place that throbs with its own heartbeat.

It's like an annoying splinter in a hard-to-reach place that throbs with its own heartbeat.

I didn't always have the problem of people making fun of me, but things changed after my parents got divorced and my family was split in two. We were on a new journey to St. Simons Island. Honestly, it was one the greatest places in the world to live, but I really did not make that many friends.

Whispers

In the beginning, I had two best friends, Lilly and Susan. Susan was at a different school, though, so that left me with only Lilly most of the time. I was so thankful for Lilly, because other girls were either too good for me or decided to make fun of me because of how skinny I was, how big my ears were, or how large my gap was. Yeah, I knew it was big, but like I said earlier, those words cut pretty deep.

On top of what others noted as physical flaws, people also made fun of me because I liked to play soccer with all the guys at gym instead of cheering on the sidelines. I hated the fact that I was a little smelly afterwards, but I loved the rush of playing and beating some of those guys. Not only did winning feel fantastic, but it also gave me a brief feeling as if nothing had changed and I was still back at home playing with *all* my brothers in the yard. It was a piece of home, and I was unwilling to give that up for a few more friends who didn't understand me or like me for who I was.

Most days I handled myself fairly well, until one day after lunch. Some girls were walking slowly behind Lilly and I; whispering, sounding like little mice trying to sneak away a tasty treat. In that moment, I did not really care what they were saying or whom they were talking about, but when we got back to the class, my friend Lilly leaned over and said in my ear, "I found out that they were talking about you when we were in the hallway. And I also heard what they were saying."

My first initial reflection was, "Well, that really isn't a surprise at all, that they were talking about me." But then I wondered, "What in the world could it have been about? They have said pretty much everything about me."

With hesitation written all over her face, Lilly continued, "They think you are bulimic." My eyes grew in astonishment. I was not sure what it meant but it did not sound good.

"What in the world is that? I have never heard of that," I said.

My sweet friend Lilly, who really could have been my sister because we looked so much alike, leaned farther and explained the definition. When she told me, I was so humiliated. I was lonely, and I missed home. I wanted to crawl into a hole and die at that point. Why would they think that about me? I would never do anything like that — ever. I hated having to face these kinds of situations at school every day but sadly, it was the norm for me.

Island Girl

Luckily, the Island — as locals called it — had more to offer than just some punk kids. When we were on the Island, I would do my best to push aside the bad and focus on the good. The best thing was when we got a twenty-four-foot white-and-blue cabin boat. I loved that thing! When we went on our day cruises or our weekend trips, I did not have to face people making fun of me or talking behind my back. I would feel the wind on my skin, the sun at my back, and the water beneath my toes, and I would let go of all my worries, drowning them in a sea of forgetfulness.

My favorite part of the boat was not all the stuff that we could do on it or with it, but all the dolphins that followed. Sometimes we would be out on the water for only five minutes before they would come out to play. Their faces would gleam with joy, and their eyes would pierce inside mine to read my every thought. They would laugh with us, play, and even let us pet their rubbery, silky skin. Whenever I was out on the water with them, just for a moment I forgot all my pain.

Some of them were bottle-nosed dolphins with white undersides, and others had pink undersides. We even got to play with some spotted dolphins. But I didn't care what kind they were; they were my closest friends because no judgment followed. They just wanted to play, and they were my safe haven.

I couldn't get enough of our dolphin adventures. I couldn't wait for the time that we would go out again and see my friends joyfully leap out of the water. I had so much fun watching them welcome us back the best way that they knew how. The best part was that as drops of water dripped beneath them, creating a ripple effect in the water below, the rolling circles would push back my horrendous memories.

Eventually St. Simons wasn't all that bad — other than all the bad mouths that were all around me at school. I was finally getting the hang of our new home. Then the unthinkable happened. Just when I was getting used to St. Simons, my mom gave my brother and me word of her new job in St.

Marys, Georgia. I couldn't believe it! We were going to have to move again. I hated the fact that I had to move again. I did not want to leave behind Lilly, Sarah, and especially the dolphins. I was happy about leaving all the people who talked bad about me and made my life miserable at the time, but I hated leaving behind all of the good.

Although, I couldn't help but ponder if maybe the new place would be better. I thought that maybe my new school would be better. Maybe, just maybe, the girls would be nicer to me in my new school. I could only cross my fingers and dream.

On The Road Again

Millions of thoughts scrambled through my brain as I sat in the backseat of our dreadful, ancient ride of an SUV, heading to another location for the second time in four years. On that bitter, cloudy, and very bumpy ride, I could not help but overthink every single waking moment I had lived up to that point of my life—both the good and the bad, playing the moments over and over in my mind like a bad country song. Now, adding to my bad song was another new school, a new town, and a new place to prove myself all over again.

All the while, my mom still held on to her optimism and was certain it was going to be the perfect place for us— our hope and our sanctuary. But then again, I wanted to go back home to St. Simons, where the salt filled the air and the smell of marsh—aka "dead fish"—lingered. Weird, I know. Everyone says that bad fish stinks after it hangs around for a while, but to me, bad fish was comfortable. Bad fish was my home away from home, away from my dad and older brothers.

"Mom, do we really have to go there? Can't we just turn back around, please?"

"We are almost there, honey. You will see—you are going to love it there," my mom said with a voice full of spunk.

Then, as we started to get closer to the St. Marys River, an unexpected delight occurred; a salty-tasting breeze leaped into my nose and into my mouth as I hung my head out of the window, trying to blow away all my negativity. Now that smelled like home to me, reminiscing back to our St. Simons Island home that we had left about an hour ago.

"I guess I could get used to this, Mom." I sounded pretty hopeful at this point in order to make her feel better, but deep down inside, I was still hurting, torn, and really wanted to give my eyes permission to turn on so they could start pouring tears like a waterfall splashing and drenching everything below.

Then I saw it: a strange building on the right side of the road that resembled a lighthouse. "Well, that is kind of weird and cool at the same time. I wonder what that is," I mumbled to myself as we whipped by quickly. I turned my body forward to close my eyes and rested my head on the back of the seat, trying to prepare myself for another life while listening to my family talk about how great things were going to be this time. "Man, I really hope they are right. I could use something great," I considered as my thoughts began to bounce into the bumps we left behind us.

Here We Go Again

That fall I started the seventh grade at St. Mary's Middle School. Eventually I made some really great friends, but in the beginning, it was really tough. As with my previous school, I got really awful looks from everyone. I could not believe how people treated new kids. People looked at me as if *everything* was my fault and I'd better own up to it, like it was my fault they got the wrong teacher for the year, or their boyfriend quit talking to them, though actually he had quit talking to them over the summer. I felt the urge to run to the bathroom multiple times throughout the first month to make sure there wasn't a booger hanging out of my nose, because of all the stares. I was so aggravated. I thought this school was going to be better. I was so wrong — *so wrong*.

In my first week of school, I encountered a girl who was a head taller than I was. She had the muscles of a tenth-grader, and man she had an attitude.Till this day, I don't even remember what I did or said to make her so angry. Frankly, I think I just looked at her. But whatever it was, she did not like it. She said, "Can I help you, little girl? Is there something I need to do *to* you? You need to turn back around before I bust you up." I had no idea what to do.

I was frozen in an ice storm of thoughts: "Should I tell someone? But if I tell someone, I will become the nark of our grade. I can't be *that* new girl." For the first time in my life, I was actually scared *for* my life. The worst part was I did not have Lilly or anyone like her yet. Once again, I was all by myself, without a soul to turn to, and I wanted to go home. But this time it wasn't the Island—I wanted my dad. I wanted my brothers. I was tired of being scared of, "Lions, and tigers, and bears! Oh, My!" Like Dorothy from the *Wizard of Oz,* I wanted to click my "bright red" heels together and shout, "There is no place like home," and show up in my bed in that beautifully pink room, back to when things were great. When my family was one and I didn't have to face these giants alone.

The fear that gripped me on a daily basis was unbearable. I had heard of bullying once before, but I never once considered it could happen to me. Now, I can whole-heartedly say that the girl never touched me, but she did not have to. The emotional drama and weight that I felt was enough to begin crushing my already fragile psyche. I thought she was going to hurt me, and that was messing me up just as much. Until I made some true friends, and even after I did, I didn't know how to act around my arch-nemesis. I was afraid that one small move or word on the wrong day was going to be "the day"—the day that she would take me out for good. I desperately needed something good to happen to get my mind off my bully. Thankfully, one day a light shined in the darkness for me.

Reflection:

Can you recall a time or times in your life when people or groups of people ripped you apart as a person? Can you recall a time in your life when you were the person or apart of a group that tore someone else down? In each of these situations how did you feel afterwards?

Scripture Focus:

Ephesians 4: 30-32, "And don't grieve God's Holy Spirit. You were sealed by Him for the day of redemption. All bitterness, anger and wrath, shouting and slander must be removed from you, along with malice. And be kind and compassionate to one another, forgiving one another, just as God also forgave you in Christ."

PART 2

A GLIMMER OF HOPE

*Life was in Him, and that life was the
light of men.
That light shines in the darkness, yet the darkness did not overcome it.*

~John 1:4-5

*Keep shining through; you may be a lighthouse
to someone trying to make it.*

~Caroline Naoroji

CHAPTER 4: MY LIGHTHOUSE

Then God said, let there be light: and there was light.

~Genesis 1:3

*I*n my mind's eye, I was sitting in the dark without any light in sight. When I tried to walk forward, I would stumble over the pebbled sidewalk made of all my doubts. I couldn't find my way around all the mess because I had lost all visibility of my feet. The path before me was blocked — until suddenly a light pierced through the darkness and I could finally see hope in front of me. I wanted to close my eyes and stay surrounded by the dark, but I couldn't. The light was drawing me in, and I couldn't resist it any longer.

Hope came to me in the form of a girl from the church that my family and I had been attending for just a short time. She invited me to this place called The Rock Bible Study at Lighthouse Christian Broadcasting. I couldn't find rest in anything else in my life, so I convinced myself, "Why not give this a shot? I have nothing to lose, right?"

I had never heard of a Christian radio station before or, better yet, one that had a Bible study at it. I was pretty fascinated by the ideal, but I was also a little nervous because I really did not know anyone there. I wondered if the people there would make fun of me too. I wondered if they would accept me for who I was on both the inside and the outside. What would they think of me? I thought, "Ahhhh, another place to prove myself. I am so tired of this vicious cycle."

When we got there, I could not believe my eyes. The Bible study was held at the building that caught my eye when my family and I first came into town, the one that actually looked like a lighthouse. The building was so amazing and unique. When I got out of the car, my legs were shaking with fear. I finally got up the courage to move from my planted position and began walking up the pathway leading to the crowd. Out of the blue, a lady came towards me. At that moment, I don't know why...I took a mental picture.

She was wearing matching clothes with someone who I guessed was her husband. She had golden-blonde hair, which curled beautifully yet uncontrollably, and out of nowhere it happened—before I could catch my next breath, she was in my personal bubble. She said, "Hey, sweetie, I have never seen you before. What is your name?" And then she hugged me—a kid she had never met before who was five feet three and weighed ninety pounds, with ears the size of an elephant whose head had not quite grown into them yet, and, of course, with gaps in her teeth. Who could forget the gaps?

I could not believe that she had hugged me. Because of that one hug, something happened to me. A breakthrough happened, much like an actual lighthouse sits on the edge of a raging sea and gracefully gives terrified seamen a glimmer of hope when they see her lights dancing in circles after a night in the darkness. Through this precious woman's embrace, I found hope. I had no idea how much I needed the hug at that exact moment in time, but I really did.

To the crowd around me, it may have looked like a simple hug from the lady who hugged everyone in sight. However, that hug represented so much to me as a little girl then, and it still holds the same weight in my heart as a woman today. The hug represented the arms of Jesus gripping me and leading me to a life that mattered, regardless of how broken I was inside.

> *The hug represented the arms of Jesus gripping me and leading me to a life that mattered, regardless of how broken I was inside.*

Now don't get me wrong. I was greatly loved by everyone in my family, but I needed a deeper love. I needed the love of Jesus, and in the midst of the stranger's hug, I found the heart of Jesus—a heart that didn't care what I looked like at all, did not care where I came from, and did not care what people had said about me in my previous life.

The woman with her arms around me was Jesus with skin on. She was my lighthouse leading me to the light source. She set aside all the junk that mattered to everyone else. All she knew was that Jesus knew who I was and wanted me to be caught in His embrace. In that moment, I was loved in the middle of my mess, and it led me to eventually accept an eternal love, the love of Jesus — a love that is unconditional from a God who embraces my imperfections.

I was a master at hiding who I really was, but when the lady from the station (I would eventually call her momma Vickie) welcomed me for who I really was, I realized that God wanted to do the same. I had done a pretty good job up until that point convincing others that I was okay, but really, I was shipwrecked inside.

I was tired of listening to all the voices around me. I may have looked different and had different interests, but that did not matter one bit. All that mattered was that I finally realized that Jesus loved me. He saw me as beautiful. He wanted me even before I was born. He fashioned me together and knew the details of my everyday life. He wasn't surprised at what I was going through. He had known that my family was going to fall apart, that those girls were going to make fun of me, and that I would go to a radio station shaped as a lighthouse and be embraced by Him in a life-changing way. He cared for me, and He was with me in a timeless way.

An Eternal God

Psalm 139:13–14 puts it beautifully for me: "For it was You who created my inward parts; You knit me together in my mother's womb. I will praise You because I have been remarkably and wonderfully made. Your works are wonderful, and I know this very well." Furthermore, it expresses in verse 16, "Your eyes saw me when I was formless; all my days were written in Your book and planned before a single one of them began."

I learned that no matter what my journey of life had brought me, nothing surprised God, and through it all, He had never left me. He loved me and had always been with me. Through this awakening, I was finally able to rest upon the shore of the Savior and embrace my mess for the first time in my life. I learned that my mess was God's way of revealing to me and everyone else the need for a Savior.

I knew that enough was enough and that I needed Him more than ever. From that moment on, I was changed. I longed to be different. I hated the way I felt over the years from being made fun of and ripped to shreds through words and some people's actions. I wanted to be the extended arms of Jesus to others that this one woman was to me.

Instead of worrying about everything that other people said about me and focusing on my problems, I let the Lord draw my attention once again to other people who felt like I did. I started to notice people sitting alone at lunch, in the gym, or on the bus. I longed to love those whom society saw as the unlovable, accepting the unacceptable, and encouraging the ones who felt like God could never love them. Throughout my middle school and high school career, this was my mission, my life song. I had no idea that the beat of my song would be at such an amazing place as a Christian radio station. My life would never be the same.

Reflection:

In your life has there been a key person or persons who have drawn you to Jesus? What drew you to these people? Were these people flawless?

Scripture Focus:

John 8: 12, "Then Jesus spoke to them again: "I am the light of the world. Anyone who follows me will never walk in the darkness but will have the light of life.""

CHAPTER 5: THE EARLY CHURCH

We rise by lifting others.

~Robert G. Ingersoll

Civil War Vet

Small drops of hot grease splattered upon my skin, burning me once again, immediately followed by the sizzling sound of amazing curly fries as they cooked in the fryer. I hated to admit it, but my favorite restaurant, Arby's, was finally ruined for me. Before, I would have found myself placing an order as my mouth watered and my taste buds screamed for just a drop of yummy goodness, but now I was the one taking the orders and preparing them.

The reason for my new job was my recent gift from my parents for my sixteenth birthday. My lovely white Geo Metro, or as I liked to call it, an "egg on wheels" or my "roller skate," forced me to take the step into wearing my big girl panties and getting a job. *I loved that car*—hated the responsibility it took to keep it, though. What kid wouldn't?

Thankfully, it cost only about thirty dollars every week and a half to fill up the tank.

The hardest part of it was that the job was not the only responsibility I had. Although it was off-season for Basketball, I still needed to practice because I was moving up to varsity. If I was going to cut it in the older grades, there was no way around it, I had to practice so I wouldn't make a fool of the team or myself.

I also did my best to keep my grades at A's, and I went to church or the radio station whenever I had a break. I was a very busy person for my age. I wasn't really bothered by it, other than the fact that I had to give up something that I loved — time spent at the station. I did not get to spend nearly as much time there as I desired.

My job at Arby's began to take its toll, because usually I was closing late with my manager who hated to close at night by herself. I remember leaving there at two o'clock in the morning once, aimlessly walking to my car, driving away like a zombie, and running a red light. My mom found out about how late I was working and grew furious. I was doing far too much for a sixteen-year-old, but I kept at it.

I did not quit at first because my mom made the manager at Arby's promise not to work me so late. It didn't really matter how little I worked or how late I worked, because the more that I worked there the more I hated the smell of grease burning. I hate it there so much and I was more than miserable, I felt as if all my dreams and desires were burning away

66

like the grease. I longed to be somewhere else, doing some-thing more. I wanted to live in a different way — on purpose, for a greater purpose. I longed for ministry.

New Opportunities

I had been going to The Rock Bible Study at the radio station for about three years on and off. I had not been able to get there every week because I did not always have a ride, but aside from being with my dad, or playing with dol-phins on St. Simons Island with my mom, the station was my favorite place in the world to be. Now that I had a car of my own, I was able to attend almost every week. Sadly, my job, school, and basketball started to build a wall between the radio station and me.

I tried to juggle school as best as I knew how in order to salvage all the A's that I was striving to keep. On top of all that, I was doing my best at a job I hated in order to keep the car so I could get to the things I loved. The hours kept piling up, and the demands were becoming too great for me. I was at a crossroads. Either I had to keep the job I despised and not get to go to the place that I loved because I was working so much, or I could quit and still not be able to go because I would not have gas money to put into my car in order to go. Something had to give. So I did all that I knew to do at that point — I begged.

I will never forget the day that I sat across from Vickie, the lady with the crazy curly hair. One day after school, I skated to the station in my little white Geo, dressed in my basketball gear as I headed to practice the dreadful layups on my own. I was tired and worn. I longed for a change.

I looked Mrs. Vickie in the eyes and cried like a little baby. I pleaded to her without taking many breaths between each sentence that came forth from my mouth: "Mrs. Vickie, please help me. I hate my job, and I am overwhelmed. I need a job to put gas in my car, and I think I want to quit basketball. My dad is going to kill me. I don't know what to do. All I know is that I love this ministry. I love being a part of everything here, helping youth, and just being here. Please help me, Mrs. Vickie. I can't take it anymore. Something has to change. Can I please work here?"

She answered me as she dragged out as long as she could my three-syllable name, as she often did to everyone's name, even if it was only a one-syllable name. "Tif-fan-y, my sweet Tiffany. I love that you love being here. I am just not sure how we can hire you right now. How much would you need to stay afloat?"

"I only need about thirty dollars a week to put gas in my car. Please, Mrs. Vickie, I will do anything. I want so badly to be here," I petitioned, as if "no" was just not an option.

She sat there for what felt like an eternity and added with a slight hesitation, "We do need someone to clean the station once a week. Do you think that is something that you would be interested in doing for us?"

I leaped from my seat while shouting, "Are you kidding me? When do I start?" I was so ready to start right then and there. But then I remembered one of the most important parts of it all and continued, "Wait! How do I tell my family that I want to quit basketball? How do I tell them that I want to quit my job? How do I convince them to let me make these major transitions in my life? Mrs. Vickie, what do I do?" She didn't know the exact words to say at that point, so she prayed for me to have wisdom and guidance. I left her side a little more confident and ready to take on the challenge of facing my parents.

After some time, I worked up the courage to have some really hard conversations with my family. I told my parents, "I hate working at Arby's, and I know that I am okay at basketball, but I am not great at it. I may not always play basketball, but ministry will always be there — it is where my heart is. Plus, the station has given me an amazing opportunity to join them." I was so surprised at their responses. My mom was totally on board with the changes. She could tell that it was where I was supposed to be. My dad was a little more difficult to convince and was upset that I wanted to quit basketball, but eventually he came around. I was free to join the ministry!

I couldn't help but think that the station was it for me — it is where I wanted to spend all my time. I believed in their ministry, and I loved to see all that God was doing there—so much so that missing The Rock Bible Study on Tuesday nights was just not an option. My heart was set.

All of a sudden, basketball wasn't important to me anymore. My friends mattered, but God mattered more. The station was my refuge, and I wanted to bring others to it so that they could see how wonderful it was, but more importantly, how great their God was, how great my God was. I could not wait to start cleaning with all the might in the world, like a Mr. Clean clone, minus the baldheadedness of course.

All In

I took great pride in my new position. To some, it may have seemed like the lowest of the lows, but honestly, it was the greatest job ever. I got to clean while I prayed and listened to great music. There was no greater feeling to me. Not only that, but I got to witness firsthand the true ministry of Jesus, how the early church operated in the book of Acts after Jesus went to be with His Father. They were a body of believers who did not have a perfect building to meet in, the greatest light show, or followers with all the bells and whistles; they just loved Jesus and each other and made sure that no one lacked anything at all.

Just like in the early church in Acts, the people at the station took me in and showed me Jesus. They helped to tend to my wounds emotionally. They prayed for me. They gave me a job. They entrusted me, a sixteen-year-old, with their ministry — a girl who loved basketball, a girl with braces, a girl who was finally growing into her ears — and accepted her for who she was inside and out. They did not look at me and tell me that I didn't belong in the family of God.

They did not tell me that I was weird because I liked to play basketball with the guys before and after The Rock and got a little sweaty. In fact, they were my biggest cheerleaders on the sidelines, telling me to beat whatever guy I could. I was fully accepted, even to the point of letting me be such a huge part of the ministry.

I may have started out cleaning the station, but that is not where I ended up. When I started working there, I never thought I would get the chance to do the things that they let me do. After I had cleaned for a little while, they asked me if I would go on the air on Saturdays from 3:00 to 6:00 p.m. I could not believe that they asked me to do that. I thought, "Are you crazy?"

I was so nervous my first time on the air. My whole body shook with terror. I could have been mistaken for a tomato with eyes that day, like Bob the Tomato from Veggie Tales; I wondered where Larry the Cucumber had run off to. Eventually I did get the hang of it, and once my confidence built, they also allowed me to host The Rock Bible Study, the live broadcast they had every Tuesday, which had been my first encounter with the station. I was humbled that they allowed me to be a part of their ministry, and I felt so alive.

As the years passed and I became a senior in high school, I was able to be more involved than ever. Luckily, I was in the work program through school, and I was able to work at the station and spend almost all my time there — my original dream. They eventually asked me to go on the air Mondays through Fridays from 1:00 to 3:00 p.m., and after a while, my time moved to 6:00–7:45 p.m. I had never thought that I would be able to go on during the week, especially as an eighteen-year-old.

One day Mr. Paul, Mrs. Vickie's husband and her fashion twin, pulled me aside and asked how I would like to go on drive time during the week from 3:00 to 6:00 p.m. I was ecstatic to take them up on their offer, but when the actual day came, I was an absolute mess. Mr. Paul said oh so gently with a huge grin on his face the first time I went on the air, "So, Tiffany, there are probably a million people listening right now. Don't screw it up." I was shaking in my skin once again.

For anyone who understands the radio world, this is pretty much unheard of and does not make any sense. Who in their right mind would put an eighteen-year-old girl, who sometimes mumbled and stumbled over her words, on the air on an FM station during drive time before she even graduated from high school? I was honestly asking the same exact question.

But the more I learned about the Lighthouse family, the more I realized that they did not trust me — they trusted the

God in me. I was no longer a "stray" per se. I was a part of the family of God. They knew that I loved Him and their ministry. They knew I wanted to do whatever I could to bring more people in to the family of God — they knew my heart.

As the Lighthouse family, the body of Christ, we did all that we could to help whomever we could with the heart of Jesus. Acts 4:32–35 reveals:

> Now the large group of those who believed were of one heart and mind, and no one said that any of his possessions was his own, but instead they held everything in common. And the apostles were giving testimony with great power to the resurrection of the Lord Jesus, and great grace was on all of them. For there was not a needy person among them, because all those who owned lands or houses sold them, brought the proceeds of the things that were sold, and laid them at the apostles' feet. This was then distributed for each person's basic needs.

Because of The Rock Bible Study and the average age of those who came to the station on a weekly basis, we mostly helped out with middle school and high school students. We did not have houses to sell or anything else that extreme to give, but we did our best to fill each other's needs. When someone needed prayer, we stopped and prayed. When someone was struggling with school, we would stop and study. If there was a need, we did our best to fill that need. We did not care what the person looked like, where they came from, what they were in the middle of, or where they were going from there. We

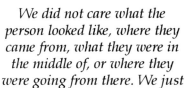

> *We did not care what the person looked like, where they came from, what they were in the middle of, or where they were going from there. We just wanted them to meet Jesus, and we wanted to meet their needs. We were of "one heart and one mind."*

just wanted them to meet Jesus, and we wanted to meet their needs. We were of "one heart and one mind."

You Lift Me Up

Who would have ever thought that a radio station, not a church, would be the picture of the early church for me and for many others touched by that ministry? We did our best to truly walk out how Jesus meant His church to be. For the Bible study, we did not need a perfect building, because for years we met on the lawn in front of the station to teach God's Word. We didn't care that the radio station wasn't big enough to hold all of us kids. We just wanted more of God and His Word, even if that meant battling the mosquitoes that tried to fight for our attention.

We didn't even fret over the afternoon storm clouds that rolled in as we set up each week. We would see storm clouds rolling towards us about to rain all over the amazing sound guys' "volunteered" expensive equipment, and we would pray and the storm clouds would dissipate. In ten years, it rained us out only twice. On the south Georgia–north Florida line, that is almost unheard of. It always rains in the afternoons—three o'clock on the dot. Three is when we had to set up the equipment for the live broadcast that started at six thirty. Luck? Not at all, my friends, but a miracle. And even more of a miracle was how the Bible study started.

The Rock Bible Study started with just four guys in the upper room of the radio station. They had a heart for youth to meet the real Jesus. They were so dedicated that they would wear Hawaiian shirts every Tuesday at school to tell people about the Bible study. They did not know how big it would grow and that it would birth other ministries such as a youth radio show, The Rock Youth Ministry as it is known today with an actual building to meet in and broadcast online to millions of people, women's groups, and much more. Those guys knew the importance of the body of Christ operating as just that in order to reach nonbelievers and welcome them into the family of God, and they were teenagers, not leading pastors of the "greatest" church on earth.

I was so grateful to be a part of the family of God and to work alongside some of the greatest human beings on the face of the planet. They truly knew what it meant to operate as the body of Christ. They reminded me of the story of Moses during the battle of Amalek, way before the church in Acts was established.

In Exodus 17, a beautiful picture is painted of the earliest church when we see Moses raising his hands to win the battle against Amalek. Whenever His hands were raised, the Israelites prevailed; whenever He lowered his hands, Israel started to lose. Moses grew tired and the church, the people, the bride of Christ, held him up. Did a building hold him up? No! Did the perfect worship team hold him up? No! Did the perfect message hold him up? No! The church, the body of Christ, held him up.

Exodus 17:13–14 reads: "As long as Moses held up his hands, the Israelites were winning, but whenever he lowered his hands, the Amalekites were winning. When Moses' hands grew tired, they took a stone and put it under him and he sat on it. Aaron and Hur held his hands up—one on one side, one on the other—so that his hands remained steady till sunset."

Lighthouse Christian Broadcasting understood the weight of this scripture. They understood that every person needed to meet Jesus. They also took it upon themselves to be the body of Christ and hold up as many people as they could while Jesus pursued each person with all the love in His heart. They knew that in order to win some battles, if not all of them, it was important to lift each other up. Through this ministry, I learned the true meaning of the body of Christ.

They held up this little girl when she needed it the most, and they still continue that today, even at a distance. I saw them in action as they were there for the hurting, the broken, and the outcasts, and I saw how they loved them with the love of Jesus. Because of them and how they ran their ministry, I was inspired at such a young age and did everything that I could to reach people for Jesus. I was on fire for God.

Reflection:

Was there ever a time in your life when the church, the body of believers, helped to fulfill your needs? Is there a time that the church, the body of believers, failed to meet your needs?

Scripture Focus:

John 17: 20-21, "I pray not only for these, but also for those who believe in Me through their message. May they all be one, as You, Father, are in Me and I am in You. May they also be one in Us, so the world may believe You sent Me."

CHAPTER 6: JUST A CARCASS

*Just as you want others to do for you, do the same
for them.*

~Luke 6: 31

As a senior in high school, I continued to feel the significance of my life song to reach those whom most people would look past. I strived to do as much as I possibly could for the kingdom of God, not because I had to, but because my passion for the Lord was unquenchable and I desperately wanted to. I worked at the station as much as I possibly could, and I also led a Bible study on Tuesday mornings at the school.

I occasionally got into arguments about Jesus with a boy in my sociology class. He was a Satanist. I begged him to seek the Lord, but he refused. If I saw him in the hallway, he would literally hiss, "Satan," and I would boldly come back with, "Jesus."

If the school had let me, I would have taken a mega-phone with me and shouted "Jesus!" throughout the hallways, holding up an "I love you" and "free hug" sign. I knew that was probably a bad idea, so I resorted to meeting people wherever they were. Out of all the things that the Lord put on my heart for that moment in time, nothing was as important to me as talking to Ricky.

A Bold Move

In order for you to understand the weight of talking to him, it is important to reflect back to the year 1999, when tragedy took place in the United States. In that year the Columbine High School massacre occurred, which was extremely devastating and made a lot of people fear sending their children to school in "safe" America. The year I was a senior was only four years after the awful event took place. So here I was, all of four years later, and here was Ricky — an out-of-town tenth-grader who stood almost six feet tall.

No one knew he was that tall, because he always walked hunched over, as if he were trying to create a cave by himself in order to shut the whole world out. His black hair was as dark as night and made its way straight down his face perpendicular to his cheekbones, slicked down to touch his collarbone exactly. His skin was beautifully tanned, but you would not notice it because of his hair, the black makeup around his eyes that marked him like a raccoon, and lips to match both his hair and the makeup on his face. His arms were hidden, and so were his legs; no matter the weather outside, he faithfully wore his long black trench coat. Ricky never talked to anyone, but he was pretty powerful. I say "powerful," but to be quite frank, he was feared. I am not kidding; whenever he would walk down the halls, people would literally split as the Red Sea had parted when Moses' staff entered the water.

Every day when I sat with my friends at lunch, I always noticed Ricky sitting by himself. He sat there with this face of complete disgust with everything around him, as if even the fabric of his clothing was bothering him, with every fiber singing his least favorite song of "Ha, ha, something is still touching you." When I saw this vision of this boy all alone for enough days in a row, I could not take it any longer. I just had to go talk to him. I was not sure whether I was brave or stupid, but I was going with full confidence that this guy was going to meet Jesus.

"Hi, I am Tiffany," I said as bubbly as I could. He did not respond at all…all I heard was crickets. All my friends thought I was crazy, but I couldn't stop. For two whole weeks, I sat with him at lunch in silence. He did not say a word, so it was quiet on his end; but since I have been known to talk a five-year-old to death, I had great conversations with myself. He just happened to hear it all. One day he did chime in with, "You are not going to go away, are you?"

I quickly responded, "Nope!" and continued with my pep talk.

One day during lunch, I was talking to him when he abruptly shouted, "*Can you please* _____ go away?" Now I am sure that it is easy for you to fill in the blank.

Then and there, I decided to leave Ricky alone for a couple of weeks. The roles were in reverse. I left him in silence. I had a hard time doing this, but I really thought he needed some space. However, the longer I stayed away, the more the Lord stirred in my heart to go back to talk to him again.

I thought the Lord was crazy. I argued, "Jesus, this kid is going to choke me!" Then I was quickly reminded that Jesus never left me alone, and I did not want to leave this boy without anyone. He was lonely, and I knew he had to miss home, just as I had many times before.

Reluctantly, I decided to go back to talk to him at his "personal circle" cafeteria table, seeing that no one else dared to talk to him. I slammed my books down with authority and said sternly, "Listen, you may not want me around, but I do not care. I am not going anywhere!" I took my seat that I claimed as my own right next to him, invading his personal bubble.

He questioned, "Why do you care so much to talk to me?"

I chuckled, "Because you seem like such a nice, fun person to talk to." We laughed together as if we both knew how untrue that statement was because of the way he portrayed himself to others around him.

To Change or Not To Change

I didn't take much time before I took a dive and invited him to The Rock, where I had embraced the real Jesus for the first time in my life not so long before. When I asked him, I could not believe my ears when he actually said yes. I was ecstatic. I just knew that it was going to be the day that Ricky encountered Jesus.

The evening that we showed up, the same lovable woman who had hugged me for the first time, Vickie, came up to Ricky and gave him a gigantic hug. I wish I would have taken a picture of his face during that moment, but since I didn't, the picture is forever ingrained in my brain. He was as stiff as a board — actually, his normal height from standing so tall. He was screaming from the inside out, *"Get. Her. Off. Of. Me — Now!"* My initial thought after that moment was that he was going to beg me to take him home, but to my surprise, he wanted to stay.

One of my favorite youth pastors spoke that night. I do not remember exactly what he spoke about, but I do remember that it was the first time that I saw Ricky really smile. When we got back to the car, he said that the speaker reminded him of his brother. I never found out why that was significant to him, but truthfully, it did not matter — Ricky had smiled!

On another weekend, I invited him to a youth rally and then a lock-in at my church to follow; that is, when youth groups still did lock-ins regularly. I thought, "Yes, this is it—he is going to get saved!" We went to the rally, and it was amazing in every way. The speakers were truly inspiring, and I thought to myself that there was no way Ricky could say no to Jesus after that service. To my surprise, he did not share anything with me that he did, but as much as I wanted salvation for Ricky I was seeing huge improvements in him. I saw him smiling more, and I am sure Jesus was too. I was thankful to meet Ricky right where he was in life and just be Jesus with skin on as much as I could.

We left the rally that evening and went straight to the church for the lock-in. As soon as we got there, my youth pastor pulled me aside. I had no idea the words that were about to come out of his mouth. He said, "Tiffany, have you noticed what is on Ricky's shirt?" I had no idea what he was talking about. I was too busy trying to show this boy the love of Jesus to notice what was on his shirt. My youth pastor continued, "He is wearing a black shirt with Marilyn Manson on a cross, and he is hanging upside down. I want you to ask him to go to the bathroom and turn it inside out. It is very offensive."

I looked at my youth pastor and refused. I was not going to have my friend—who needed the love of Jesus—to switch his shirt around just because it was offensive to the pastor. How would that benefit Ricky? Because that was who it was about, right? He obviously wore it on purpose to see what people would say. I did not understand the purpose behind flipping the shirt.

If we asked him to turn it inside out, my fear was that he would be pushed from the church for the rest of his life, and I could not let that happen over a shirt. I wanted Ricky to see the real Jesus — the Jesus who is not easily offended and is slow to anger. I didn't ask Ricky to turn his shirt that day, and I am glad I didn't because I continued to see a huge change.

The more I hung out with Ricky, the more I saw him smile, because Jesus was doing amazing things in his heart. He even began to change his outward appearance all on his own, without force. The makeup was washed from his face, his trench coat disappeared, he started to wear colors other than black, and he actually cut his hair super short so that you could see his perfectly tanned face without any interference. Ricky was transforming beautifully before my eyes.

I knew that he was changing on the inside, but I loved seeing an outward change, because oftentimes you do not get to see that happen for a person. He even started forming other friendships, and you could tell that he was gaining more confidence within the school. I was so proud of him.

Sadly, after a while, we quit hanging out together as much. It was not really for any particular reason; it is just what happens in high school, I guess. But there were no hard feelings at all. Every now and then, we would catch each other's eye as we walked down the hall, and we would smile. He looked happy, and that made me extremely happy.

I graduated from high school and never saw Ricky again, so I do not know where he stood with the Lord. However, before I left school, he did give me a letter, and I was shocked at the words written so plainly before me. His words were these:

> *Tiffany, I just wanted to say thank you for being consistent in talking to me. I just wanted you to know that I used to be a dedicated Christian, serving the Lord in the church. Something happened at church and people were not very nice, and I got completely turned away by all of it. . . .*

I could not believe the words in front of me. When you looked at Ricky before his outward transformation, you would have never guessed that he used to be a devoted follower of Christ. And I am not talking about the clothes he wore or the makeup he worked so hard to fashion together; everyone is different and has his or her own style. The main issue was the appearance on his face; it was pure depression underneath it all.

Another thing quickly came to the surface of my mind: what had been so bad as to turn him away from the church? A better question would be why hadn't anyone sought him when he left the church? How could the church turn its face from such a young boy who literally transformed into someone who hated everything around him? My heart ached for him, and I was so thankful and humbled that God chose me to help bring him back to a portion of the person he was before.

A Rude Awakening

I wish I could say that I treated everyone I connected with in my early ministry or even in my late ministry this way, seeking all the hurting with everything as Jesus did, but I can't say that I did. You see, right before I am tempted to pat myself on the back about Ricky, I am quickly reminded by the Lord of a young girl at the radio station named Stacy.

Stacy came to The Rock Youth Ministry for many weeks in a row. She stood five feet three inches tall and was a very timid person. She spoke so softly that if too many distractions were present, I had to lean in really far in order to hear her well. She had round cheeks, tanned skin, and black hair almost as dark as Ricky's. She came to The Rock every week, and for months that led into years, we spoke about the same things she struggled with. She had relationship problems, anxiety problems, and nothing was ever going to get better for her, so she claimed. Eventually I got to the point that whenever I saw Stacy walking up to the station building, I would quickly get into conversations with other people just so I would not have to talk to her.

I would brush her off with a quick "What's up?" and my finger held in the air as if I were tipping an old cap. I was tired of hearing the same stories over and over again. I was tired of giving advice that never seemed to change her, or so I thought. I was desperate. I wanted to shake her and shout, "Wake up and snap out of it, sister! Believe the Bible and move on already." I would like to say that I ditched her only a couple of times, but this went on for quite a while. After some time passed, she quit coming to The Rock. I mean, who could blame her, right?

Why did I push her away? Why didn't I seek her out and continue to help her? The biggest problem is, I have no idea how the way I treated her affected her or where she ended up in life. I will have to answer to that one day. My prayer was always that Jesus would shine through me, that when people looked at me, they would see the face of Jesus because I would step aside. I was determined to be the hands and feet of Jesus. But when it came to Stacy, I failed miserably.

The Lord started to convict me and cautioned me to be careful with the way that I treated people. Oftentimes as a

But Jesus never leaves anyone high and dry.

Christian, it is easier to brush people off and get tired of hearing the same things from them. But Jesus never leaves anyone high and dry. He does not give up on anyone. He never gave up on me. I was driving to a friend's house one day when the Lord revealed this to me through something I never thought He could use—a dead animal.

I saw the dead animal on the side of the road as I approached, and I could not stop myself from looking at the animal: looking away . . . looking at the animal . . . looking away. There was something about it that made me want to see how bad the hit really was — *sick, I know!* I felt bad for the animal, but all I could do was stare at the pain. Then, as I approached the animal, got one more glance, and turned away, the Holy Spirit spoke to me. He said, "Be careful that you do not treat people this way." My first thought was, "Lord, what are You talking about? That does not make any sense at all — that was a dead animal, not a person." But over the course of a week, it started to sink in.

The Lord showed me that when people are hurting, lost, need support, or whatever the case may be, a lot of times it is easier to just look at these people . . . look away . . . look at these people . . . look away. The thought may cross my mind, "Man, that looks really bad. I will pray for them," but then I just drive away. And if I am honest with myself, half the time I do not even stop to pray. In addition, I do not think for a second to actually stop to check to see whether these people are "still breathing," nor do I try to fulfill the need that they may have at that present time. Instead, I just say I will pray for them and move on. Now, I am not saying that prayer is a bad thing; it is the most powerful thing that I can do as a Christ follower. However, this is not where Jesus wanted me to stop. He longed to use me to encourage those around me, fulfill their needs, and to make certain that no one around me would be in need in any way.

The Lord brought me to 1 John 3:16–20:

> This is how we have come to know love: He laid down His life for us. We should also lay down our lives for our brothers. If anyone has this world's goods and sees his brother in need but closes his eyes to his need — how can God's love reside in him? Little children, we must not love with word or speech, but with truth and action. This is how we will know we belong to the truth and will convince our conscience in His presence, even if our conscience condemns us, that God is greater than our conscience, and He knows all things.

When I read this passage, I immediately thought of the parable of the good Samaritan in Luke 10:25–37. Jesus was approached by a lawyer who wanted to test Him and asked about the law concerning eternal life: "Teacher, what must I do to inherit eternal life?" (verse 25). Jesus then asked the man how he read it, and the man responded, "Love the Lord your God with all your heart, with all your soul, with all your strength, and with all your mind; and your neighbor as yourself'" (verse 27). Jesus told the man that he was correct, and that if he did this, he would live. The man wanted to know more, so he asked further, "Who is my neighbor?" (verse 29). Jesus then told an interesting story that anyone can relate to.

Jesus proceeded to tell of a man who traveled from Jerusalem to Jericho and was attacked by robbers. They took everything from him, beat him, and left him almost to the point of death. Three different people passed the man: a priest, a Levite, and a Samaritan. The priest and the Levite ignored the man as a dead carcass on the side of the road. But the Samaritan stopped to see if the man was still alive.

I can't imagine how bad this man looked, but he was bad enough to have wounds that needed to be healed. The Samaritan did not just pass by and throw money at the man or tell him, "Get it together, brother, and move on already. So what, you got beat down. Get over it, and leave the place you are in." No, he took time with the man to meet him where he was, to be Jesus with skin on, and to show the man true compassion.

Verses 34 and 35 explain further: "He went to him and bandaged his wounds, pouring on oil and wine. Then he put the man on his own donkey, brought him to an inn and took care of him. The next day he took out two denarii and gave them to the innkeeper. 'Look after him,' he said, 'and when I return, I will reimburse you for any extra expense you may have.'"

Jesus said all these things and then, in verse 36, followed with, "Which of these three do you think was a neighbor to the man who fell into the hands of robbers?" In verse 37, the expert in the Law replied, "The one who had mercy on him." Jesus told him, "Go and do likewise" (verse 37).

In this scripture, Jesus laid it out so simply to me. As a Christian, I am called to go above the call of duty. I am supposed to go the extra mile for people. I am taught in Matthew 5:41 that "if anyone forces you to go one mile, go with them two." I am not supposed to treat people like they are dead carcasses on the side of the road — wounded and something I try to stay away from instead of trying to patch their wounds, and saying, "Oooohhhh, that looks bad. Someone should take care of that!" I started to realize, through the teaching of Jesus and the Holy Spirit, that I needed to start taking responsibility for not only myself, but also for others in the world around me — no matter how hard it was, how much it cost me, or how messy it got.

The "Take Off"

Because of this knowledge, I was ready to take my relationship with the Lord to the next level. I longed to explore the "depths of the sea" and give my future to Him. In the words of my all-time favorite band, Audio Adrenaline, I wanted to be His "hands and feet." I wanted so much to stay at the radio station and continue doing ministry with them because I had learned so much, but I knew that I needed to grow more and train some on my own. I decided to extend the ministry that the Lord put on my heart by going to a non-accredited, nine-month go-to-grow program at Texas Bible Institute.

I knew it would be hard because I would not be with my family, but I knew it was necessary. I was so excited to go, and I just knew that it was going to be a good thing. I knew that the Lord was going to grow me in so many ways. I felt like it was going to be a launching pad for a deeper relationship with Him and open doors for more ministry opportunities for His glory, but honestly, it was anything but that. Through a series of events I became an accidental Pharisee.

Reflection:

Has anyone in your life gone out of his or her way to make you feel accepted? Have you every gone out of your way to make a person or persons to feel accepted?

Scripture Focus:

Hebrews 13:2, "Don't neglect to show hospitality, for by doing this some have welcomed angles as guests with out knowing it."

Part 3

MASQUERADE

And after all, what is a lie? Tis but the truth in a masquerade.
~Alexander Pope

Don't lie.
Life is a puzzle and we are all unique pieces.
When you lie, you make it impossible to find your
true place in the grand design.
~Dr. Steve Maraboi
Unapologetically You: Reflections on Life and the
Human Experience

CHAPTER 7: ACCIDENTAL PHARISEE

God simplifies. The devil complicates.

~Elizabeth Christopher

Singer/songwriter

y alarm sounded, as it had many times in previous days, before the sun broke into its usual song. I grabbed my running shoes and headed into the bitter-cold hallway to stretch my body before another brutal thirty minutes. I thought to myself, "Man, I am so thankful that I hushed the beeping sound before the other girls heard it. I do not need any more reasons for them not to like me."

My time at Bible school was not all that I thought it would be. I was just thankful that not all the girls in my room hated me. A few of them seemed to really care about me as a person, but four out of the seven loathed me. I really didn't understand where all the hostility came from. Maybe it was from the first day, orientation day. I came with many hopes of making lifelong friends, but I was in for a rude awakening, for sure.

On orientation day, I was thrilled. I was finally getting to live another part of my dream. Many times before, I had come to camp here during the summer with my brother's youth group. The camp was where I had officially accepted Jesus into my heart at just thirteen years old after my first encounter with Him at the radio station. Texas was hardly one of my favorite places, but the camp held a special place in my heart.

At camp, I was able to worship freely without any judgment and grow in knowledge. I could play basketball like one of the guys, and it didn't matter that I was a girl. They cared only that I could play like one of them, and that gained me a lot of respect, from the guys at least. I also got to bond with my brother and his wife, so it was just a precious place of memories for me. I had longed to go to the Bible Institute ever since that first summer-camp experience. Here I was, five years later, ecstatic to dedicate nine months of my life to grow more than I ever had grown before.

When I showed up at Texas Bible Institute after a long sixteen-hour trip, I had no idea how much space I *wasn't* going to have. I had packed far too much. There were four bunk beds to each room, meaning that eight girls had to share a room, a closet, and a small shower and sink. I had never had to share a room with so many girls for an extended period of time. I had grown up with brothers, so I had never really operated well or gotten along with many girls, considering all the mean ones I had encountered throughout my young life. But I was hopeful and thought to myself, "How hard can it really be?"

I was able to unpack most of my things on the top right corner of my allotted space before we had to make a mad dash to orientation. I just knew that this was going to be my year. God was going to do something amazing in me and everyone else around me. They opened with worship, and it reminded me immediately of my camp days. I forgot that I was sixteen hours from home and worshiped as if nothing had changed.

Once worship was over, all the students were called to the altar. The pastor and founder of the organization got up to speak to inspire us. After he had said a few words, he looked at me and pointed me out. He stood above six feet tall, with hair white as snow and a smile that could go on for days.

"Hey there, young lady. What is your name?" he said, with rosy-red cheeks from getting fired up about Jesus.

"My name is Tiffany, sir," I said hesitantly, as if I had almost forgotten my name.

"Tiffany from where?" he continued.

"I am from Georgia," I said boldly that time, scaring myself with the outburst I gave.

"Well, Tiffany from Georgia, you better hold on, honey, because God's got some amazing plans for you," he declared, as if he had already had a glimpse of my future.

I wished, "Man, if only he could share the future with me in detail, then maybe I would be more prepared."

Conflict

Immediately after orientation, we had dinner, but I didn't want to hang out with anyone. I just wanted to run off to the basketball court, where I felt like I belonged. I wanted to get the feeling of hugs from my brothers, a piece of home. Honestly, it was where I felt safest, where I felt the most clarity and most alive. I spent most of my free time there, even if it meant taking multiple showers a day; the courts were where I wanted to be.

I tried to get some of the other girls to go play with me, but they refused. They seemed to care more about flirting with the guys instead of playing basketball with them. I did my best to get along with all of the girls, but we did not have much in common. The only thing that we had in common was our love for the Lord and sharing a room. When we started out, that was enough, but as time went on, we started to fight a lot.

They started to call me the goody-goody of the group because I did not cuss, studied the Scriptures a lot, and worked on homework as much as I could. Was I perfect? Absolutely not! But for some reason, things in the room started to be my fault. They started to blame silly things on me and get mad at me for no reason. They would blame me for how the bathroom looked, or for leaving my shoes on the floor though someone had just kicked them into the way, or for taking up too much space in the closet although I had the fewest clothes of everyone. They made it seem like I thought I was better than they were, but I didn't feel like that at all.

At the heart of it all, if they'd given me a real chance, they would have found out that I was my own worst enemy. Normally, I would tear myself down more than anyone else could, but I didn't because they did enough of that for me. As I found myself in a girl hurricane of emotional conflict, I realized that in girl world, life was a complicated mess, and everything was a competition. I did not think that could happen at a Christian school, but it seems that it can happen in that atmosphere even more than in the secular world.

The Best Of The Best

We were challenged daily by the best speakers across the country to do life better for Jesus. In the midst of that and being caught up in girl drama, my life quickly became extremely stressful; everything became about trying to be better than the person next to me rather than just focusing on the one who mattered the most — Jesus. There was a constant battle going on with things such as who was the skinniest, who dressed the best, who learned the most Scripture, who got on the praise team, who took better care of her body, and whom the pastor picked to pray. The list went on and on.

I wasn't okay with being second best. I desired to be all that I could be in body, mind, and spirit. I started to be very strict on myself about everything I did each day. I made sure I wasn't wasting any time on empty things. I read my Bible a lot, and I took pride in running cameras for the camera crew for camp retreats that we held for youth all over America. In my spare time, I was trying to learn guitar, and I made the conscious choice not to eat all the fatty foods at mealtimes.

I even contacted a guy who was a worker at the school and he was also a personal trainer. I was working out as much as I could. I was going nonstop all the time. My morning jogs were just part of my exercise regimen. I started to run in order to be healthier, but that is not why I continued. After months of pushing myself harder than I had ever pushed myself in my entire life, I was spent. But that was not going to keep me from running. I had to prove that I was the best.

One day, after I got my body warmed up for my morning jog, I walked to the pavement, ready to go. I started to jog at my normal pace up the mile-long stretch of road to the entryway to the school buildings. It was just barely lit, and I could hardly see my feet landing on the surface. I tried to ignore the talk about the wolves that people had sometimes spotted early in the morning and focus only on the rhythm my feet were making as they hit the pavement. I was put at ease when I saw deer galloping nearby.

As I increased my stride to run more quickly, my feet pounded like drums beating faster and faster, striving to reach my goal to finish strong. But to my surprise, instead of maintaining my normal faster pace, my body began to give out and I started to go slower. Was my body getting weaker instead of stronger? How could this be? I couldn't give up; I had to keep going. My legs were just tired — that was all.

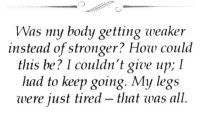

Was my body getting weaker instead of stronger? How could this be? I couldn't give up; I had to keep going. My legs were just tired — that was all.

Back In The Day

As my legs decided they couldn't keep up, I felt defeated, much as I had in my ninth-grade year of high school when I had run track. I was a puny little girl without a lick of muscle going against track stars who had been on track teams since they could walk. At my first meet, I put my feet into the blocks, and I was shaking uncontrollably. I was even more nervous because I was all alone. The only people I had to watch me were my teammates. They cared for me, but they were not family. In moments like this, I liked to picture Jesus literally right beside me. Even though I had this picture in my mind, it still hurt sometimes to be alone, especially at my first track meet.

During my first year my coach put me on hurdles of all things. I will never understand why. I guess he thought the long, lanky legs gave me an advantage — either that or he was just trying to fill the spot. Regardless, I loved my coach. He was inspiring, he cared, and he cheered for me as loudly as he could.

My feet were in the blocks, and I was as ready as I was ever going to be. The shot sounded, and I began to run with all my might. My kick got faster and faster, and somehow I was in first place as I charged around the curb. We were running the three hundred meters, and I was excited because the hurdles were shorter and much more manageable to jump over. I couldn't believe my eyes. I glanced over my right shoulder to find no one around me. I was in the lead.

I was on the last hurdle around the back end of the curb with only about a hundred meters left. I went to jump over the hurdle and got my first leg over it, but then something terrible happened. My back leg hooked the hurdle. I learned something harsh that day. I learned that practice hurdles were curved and moved when you hit them, but race-day hurdles were square at the bottom and did not move. Instead, they moved the person running—or in my case, crashing— to the ground. These hurdles did not move, and I went straight down to the ground. I was mortified, lonely, and just wanted to lie there with my face down to the ground in hopes that I would wake up from some unwanted nightmare. Instead of lying there, I dusted myself off and finished the race—dead last.

Major Concerns

Now I was in Bible school, away from family, and I had come so far. I couldn't give up. I had to keep running my hardest. I did not want to fall and fail like I had done in the ninth grade and so many times before in other areas of my life. I wanted to keep running and keep the momentum, but I just couldn't. My body felt weaker instead of stronger, which was not my original intention. What had I done to myself? I could tell that I was getting smaller, because my clothes were getting looser, but I didn't think it was that big of a deal. However, when my mom came to visit me, I knew I was not okay.

When I first heard my mom was coming to see me, I could hardly stand it. I was excited to see someone, a familiar face from home. I had been at the school for quite a while and was unable to leave. Luckily, I had found out that one of my cousins lived near the campus so once before, I was able to go to her house. But on all the other weekends, I was left behind as many others left to visit their families.

Most of the people from the school, including the girls in my room, were from Texas. Either they would go home with each other, or they would go home by themselves. I was invited only twice to go home with them, every other time I was excluded from their journeys home. I spent a lot of my weekends by myself, without a friend, just reading my Bible. Yes, the Word was very important to me, but I needed community, and I was lacking it greatly.

I couldn't wait to see my mom, and I was so happy to get out of there with her. However, I was also really nervous to see my mom after so much time had passed. I wondered if she would notice how small I was getting. I hoped that my baggy clothes would cover it up, but truth be told, I think it gave away how poor my health really was. When I first saw her smiling face change from excitement to frowns, I knew that she was concerned, but she quickly smiled again to cover her concern.

I was so glad to see her thick black hair blowing wild and crazy in the wind, to catch a smell of her favorite perfume, and, most importantly, getting her hug. I needed that hug so much, just like I had needed the hug from Vickie at the station. I had been isolated for so long. Luckily, we did not have to stay at the college. My cousin let us stay with her so that we could have a warm bed and get away from the bunk beds and drafty hallways. A warm bed...ah...I thought I was in heaven.

My mom and I talked fluff for a few days until we went shopping together during our trip. I started picking out my normal-size clothing of medium shirts and size 6-8 pants, and was shocked that none of them fit. I started to try on different sizes until I finally got to the size I was in. "A size zero, really?" I stressed to myself. I could not believe I was in a zero. I looked at myself in the mirror, bare, which is something you do not often get to do when sharing an open room with seven other girls.

I hardly recognized myself. You could see my bones sticking out of my shoulders. I had always been small, but muscular. All of my muscle had disappeared. I started to weep. I could not believe what I had done to myself. I had just wanted to take care of my body, mind, and spirit, but in the midst of striving for perfection, I became so frail, so sick. The tears overwhelmed my face.

I shouted to my mom with disgust, "Mom! Do I really look that bad?"

She lovingly said, "Honey, you look nothing like yourself. You have no muscle. I am extremely worried about you, sweet girl. You do not look like my daughter. Honey, you need help...and you need it now!"

I knew that I needed help. I could not continue the path that I was on, but I had to finish what I had started. I could not let anyone know that I was being defeated. I was so scared for other people to find out. My mom, extremely worried, did her best to convince me to go home, but I refused. I would not give up. I had to finish the race that I had started. Since she could not convince me to return home, she called the school office to have them give me two weeks away at my cousin's so that I could try to work through some stuff. However, I needed longer than two weeks; I just didn't know it at the time.

The two weeks away were glorious. I did not have people picking at me and blaming me for things, and I wasn't caught up in "girl world" drama. Once the two weeks were over, I was very upset that I had to go back to the school, but I wanted to finish—I had to. My cousin reluctantly dropped me off and let me know that if I needed anything, she would always be there for me.

I was thankful for the extension of her love, but I wasn't going to need it for very long. Our spring break came pretty fast, and it was my first trip home since I had hit rock bottom, which for me came in the form of a size zero. I was really nervous to see my family and friends and hear all that they would have to say about me.

When I saw my dad for the first time, he did what he always did: he hugged me. I know to him I probably felt like I could break in his arms, but he did not mention a thing. Then the situation got heated. Some of my family begged me to stay home. I mean, who wouldn't have? I know I looked terrible. Regardless of what anyone said to me, though, I didn't want to quit because I was afraid of what my "friends" back at school would say if I did. Even more than that, I didn't want it to be one more thing that I started and did not finish. I just couldn't let myself down. More importantly to me, I couldn't let God down.

But one night the decision was made for me. When I was staying at my dad's house, I started having an awful pain in my side. I had never felt this type of pain before. The pain would not let up, so I had to go to the ER. My dad did his best to keep his cool while we waited, and I just grumbled in my pain. He would pat my leg every now and then and remind me that everything was going to be fine.

They finally got me in the back, and after a few scans, they found kidney stones. I decided right then and there in my pain that it was a sign from God that I needed to stay home. I knew I needed help. I was not going to be okay on my own. I needed my family. I needed community. My regimen had started to break me down little by little. I was weak, I was broken, and I had to stop running.

Reflection:

Has there ever been a time in your life when you took striving for excellence a little too far? This can be in your every day life, in your relationship with Christ, or both.

Scripture Focus:

Matthew 23: 5-7, "They do everything to be observed by others: They enlarge their phylacteries and lengthen their tassels. They love the place of honor at banquets, the front seats in the synagogues, greetings in the marketplaces, and to be called 'Rabbi' by people."

CHAPTER 8: THIN CAGE

There were bars everywhere I turned.
I was trapped.

~Tiffany Wasson

I stepped on the scale for the sixth time that day, wondering why the numbers were not changing at all: 114. I could not believe that I gotten down to 114 pounds. I had always had an athletic type of body. When I played basketball in high school, they forced us to take weight lifting so that our bodies could take the grueling process of practices and games. I had done my best to keep my athletic physique, but that dwindled quickly in Texas. I wanted to change, to gain weight, and to be back to my normal weight of 135, but I was too scared. I was in far too deep. I needed help as quickly as possible.

In the beginning of my long journey to recovery, my brother Tim and his wife, the ones I had gone to camp with, let me stay with their family for a few months while I decorated my room at my dad's house. They had always been inspirations to me in my faith, and I admired the way that they lived their lives. I trusted them greatly. They did their best to teach me how to eat right, exercise correctly, and not stress over things too much.

I didn't understand the mind trap I was in. I was 18 years old and I knew how to take care of myself, but for some reason, I was like a toddler trying to learn to walk for the first time. I was in straight rehabilitation mode. I would go to the YMCA with my sister-in-law, and we would work out. She would cook me healthy meals in between and encourage me spiritually.

Once my room was completed, with the help of my sister-in-law's expertise in decorating, I moved in with my dad and Marie in Albany, Georgia, about three hours from my mom and the radio station. I signed up for college and got a job at the YMCA, once again to pay for the gas for my "roller skate." My dad and Marie were really great because they did not want me to worry about anything but gas. They paid for insurance, food, and extra things that I wanted to do.

I did my best to get back to normal quickly and to take part in a normal life, but a lot of days I truly struggled to be okay simply with who I was and where I was in life. I felt like a failure almost every day. I even started to go to counseling, but honestly, the counselor just made me feel worse. I felt like every time I made any kind of advancement, she made me feel like I was still in the place I was whenever I first went to her. I felt like I was never moving forward, which started to affect me greatly. I thought to myself, "I can't even succeed in a counseling session. How in the world am I to defeat anorexia?" My cage of perfectionism was weighing on my mind and my body, and it was continuing to starve me spiritually as well.

Overwhelmed With Perfection

I could not even write a school paper without freaking out. I remember sitting on the floor many times at night, trying to write a paper without fault from start to finish for English class. If I couldn't do it or think it through in my mind, I would break down, bury my head in the carpet, and cry until I couldn't cry anymore. My dad and mom did all they could to encourage me, but for some reason, I just felt like I was not ever going to be good enough for myself, or for anyone else, for that matter. My mind went to downhill fast, and my body cage just kept getting smaller.

I wanted my body to be flawless, so I paid close attention to everything that I ate. When I splurged on a food such as a brownie, I would do my best to count the calories. If I ate a brownie with ice cream that counted up to six hundred calories, I would be very strategic about going to the YMCA and running until I saw six hundred calories burned flash before my eyes in bright-green numbers on the treadmill. I would not leave until I saw that—it just had to be done.

My stepmom, Marie, would try to convince me that I wasn't fat. She would measure the circumference of my stomach; legs, arms, and chest to prove to me number wise that I was in good shape. She would take me shopping to show me the size that I was in to remind me that I hadn't "let myself go." She was doing all that she could in a loving way, but nothing was going to change my mind. I thought I was a ragged, imperfect mess, and I hated it—every bit of it.

The midnight hours were some of my worst moments. The TV would still be on after hours to just burn energy adding "dollars due" to my parent's bill. Suffering from insomnia, I would stare aimlessly at the television screen, thinking about the ice cream, peanuts, and chocolate syrup calling my name from the freezer and pantry. I would pry myself from my comfy daybed and tiptoe my way to the kitchen so that no one would hear me or see what I was doing in the dark.

I would scoop the ice cream, then pour the peanuts and chocolate syrup on top, and eat it. I *loved* that snack, but I would feel so guilty afterwards because I had not been able to control myself. Sometimes I felt guilty to the point that I would go back and get more. I would think, "Well, I have already done it. I've let myself go, so why stop now?"

One night the guilt was too much for me. I couldn't take it anymore. I had gone back so many times that there was no way I could count all the calories. What if I gained weight? What if I didn't run enough the next day and someone found out my dirty secret and knew what I was doing in the midnight hours when I was alone? I was ashamed. I might as well have worn a scarlet *U* on my chest when I went into public places to represent "unable to control herself" and be stoned for my horrible deeds.

The guilt was too heavy to bear, and I made my way to the bathroom. I stood over the john and prepped myself to get rid of all that I had just eaten. Then I finally did it. After many minutes passed, I became what some girl had spoken over me as a sixth-grader: I was officially a bulimic. I wanted the body of the women at the gym, but the women at the gym and in the magazines had more control over themselves then I did. They never slipped up and ate the junk that I ate, at least that is what I told myself. I had to be better. I hated throwing up, but at that point, I thought there was no other way.

Forgetting The Truth

I didn't fall into the trap of regurgitation very often, but when I did do it, I felt overwhelming guilt and shame and told myself that I would never do it again. I really wish I could say that I kept those promises to myself, but I can't. My bulimia held on for quite a while. I had forgot the words that Paul said in 1 Corinthians 6:19–20: "Don't you know that your body is a sanctuary of the Holy Spirit who is in you, whom you have from God? You are not your own, for you were bought at a price. Therefore glorify God in your body."

My body was no longer something to worship the Lord with by taking great care of it. My body became something that I could control and put into the cookie-cutter image of every other hot body out there in the world. The Lord would gently bring to my attention that it doesn't profit anything to take care of the body so much, because it is only for a short time; it is dust, a vapor, and it isn't worth putting in so much time and effort. First Timothy 4:8 reveals, "For the training of the body has a limited benefit, but godliness is beneficial in every way, since it holds promise for the present life and also for the life to come."

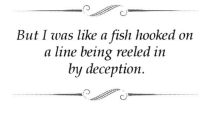

But I was like a fish hooked on a line being reeled in by deception.

But I was like a fish hooked on a line being reeled in by deception. I thought that I was bringing honor to the Lord by striving to be perfect. In reality, I was destroying everything the Lord had built in me — and it took me less than a year to do it. I started the year with a longing to grow in mind, body and spirit but now I had no respect for my body, my mind, or my spirit. I believed I was in control, and that was all that mattered. I wanted to have the best body I could have, and no one was going to stop me — no one.

Reflection:

Can you think of a time in your life when you felt trapped in a situation and couldn't gain freedom? How did you feel? Did you want to give up on everything?

Scripture Focus:

John 8: 32, "You will know the truth, and the truth will set you free."

CHAPTER 9: WAKE-UP CALL

There's a ringing in my ears
and it's my wake up call
God gave me a wake up call

~Relient K
Wake Up Call

y family did all that they could to get to me, but I wasn't that easy to get to. My mind was made up on how I was going to be. I was having a hard time listening to everyone around me. The Lord needed to get through to me, and He started to on a weekend I went home to visit my mom. I had been away from home for a while and needed a taste of what I will always consider my hometown, regardless of the number of times I've moved.

Luckily for me, it was Fourth of July weekend. There is no better place to be on the Fourth than St. Marys, Georgia. There is the best parade by the water and familiar faces, all down by the St. Marys River right across from Cumberland Island, one of my favorite places in this world. I decided that

I had been away for too long from my mom and those at the radio station. I was longing for the hugs I had missed from My mom, momma Vickie, and all of my friends.

My first attempt to see all my friends was at a softball game close to all of the action for the Fourth with the young adults group that had formed at the station. The group was called *Hebrews*, another group that was a product of those four boys and their Bible Study 10 years previous.The name was based on Hebrews 10:25: "not staying away from our worship meetings, as some habitually do, but encouraging each other, and all the more as you see the day drawing near."

When I first drove up in my famous egg car, I parked and looked in the mirror at the dark circles under my eyes, and I tightened my short pigtails on each side of my head. They were short because a woman had butchered my hair before I left to go home. Once again I got out of my car hesitantly, as I had done coming home for the first time from Texas, wondering what things people would say about my size. But those thoughts quickly dissipated when I saw . . . him.

His hands hugged the fence as he leaned in towards his team on the field, cheering them on as some of them circled the bases. He proceeded to pop some gum, and the air from within fogged up the frames of his black Oakley glasses. His legs were intertwined, and of course his shirt was off — it was July in South Georgia, for crying out loud. Long story short, he looked pretty good to me. I swallowed the lump in my throat and proceeded to say hello to everyone else. I had never seen him before and had no idea who he was, but I wanted to know. Avoiding him and pretending that I did not care one bit, I took the field to play.

A Glimpse Of Me

A little bit of my old self came out that day once the three o'clock shower decided to show its familiar face. We were not bothered by it one bit because it offered a great break to our overheated bodies. Rapidly the mud started to form on the field as I went up to bat and took the position. I squinted my eyes, fighting back the sun showing off between the thundering clouds above, since I had left my glasses at home. The ball came towards me like a floating grenade, and as I swung, I closed my eyes, hoping that I would make contact. I stayed there until I heard my best friend, Breanne, yell, "Tiffany, you actually hit it! *Ruuuuuun!*"

I couldn't believe I had hit the ball, with how weak I was, but the hit turned into a double. I rounded first base and ran to second, and as I made my way to second, I slid into the mud as if I were diving into the ocean. I was covered from head to toe in mud, and it felt great. I couldn't remember the last time that I had laughed so hard. I felt refreshed. I felt alive. I felt like a kid again.

We finished our game as best as we knew how and took a break to have the best summer treats: grilled hamburgers and hot dogs. After we were done eating, I walked over to grab my keys to leave, and the impossible happened. *He* came to talk to me. The Hebrews crew was talking about plans for the Fourth of July evening. Then his voice broke through the conversations surrounding us. "Hi, I'm Jeremy. What are you doing tonight for the Fourth? My buddy John and I were going to go downtown. Do you want to join us?"

I had a very hard time answering back right away. Why would he talk to me, especially with the way that I looked? I was confused. I answered back reluctantly, "I usually go downtown too. Truthfully, it is my favorite time and place of the year. I would love to go down there with you guys."

Even though I was shocked that he had talked to me, I rushed back home, took down my hair, showered, and got freshened up. I had never been so concerned with the way I looked before. Sure, I had my issues, but this was different. I hoped he would like my outfit and my hair — my horrible cut-off boy hair — and that he would like me. I had had boyfriends before, but this guy wasn't the same. He made me feel different even in the short time that we had talked. I didn't just feel like this was a night out with friends. I knew that deep down he was supposed to be mine. He was God's plan for me. But I thought to myself, "Seriously, Tiffany, you just met the guy."

I took one more glance in the mirror and headed back downtown. I drove up in my Geo Metro with my stepsister, who at this point I just called my "sister" and our friend Steve. We were blasting Aerosmith's "I Don't Want to Miss a Thing" and shouting the lyrics from the top of our lungs. I looked outside my window and saw Jeremy. He was wearing an American Eagle collared shirt that was pink and dressed with blue stripes, along with khaki shorts. He was sporting his Oakley glasses again and a hat.

I walked up to him wearing my blue-green American Eagle shirt and khaki shorts. A quick thought passed, "Man, we even dressed alike—I knew this was meant to be." I walked up to him with confidence, and the first thing he did was to burn my arm with a freshly burned-out sparkler. I wondered, "Okay, love at first burn?" I couldn't believe that he had burned me during our first hangout—what a jerk! But as the night went on, I saw a totally different side to him.

We left our cars at the baseball field and decided to walk downtown because traffic was horrendous, and we also figured we could get out of there faster. John, Jeremy, my sister, Steve, and I headed on our way. We got the chance to see all kinds of friends, share some treats, and catch a seat down by the river in the perfect spot to see fireworks after the sun went down.

The fireworks were beautiful as they lit up the night sky. In the exact moment that I saw the dancing lights above and as I sat next to Jeremy, I realized how tired I was of living in the masquerade I was caught in. I was tired of living a lie, pretending I was perfect. All the things I was doing were not bringing true peace to my life. But in that moment, I was at peace. I couldn't remember the last time I had been that happy, as I sat next to the man who was changing me already.

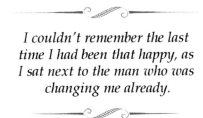

I couldn't remember the last time I had been that happy, as I sat next to the man who was changing me already.

We started to head back to our cars, and we could hear the thunder rolling in the distance. "Oh, great. We are going to get caught in the shower," I grumbled. I don't know why I was surprised. Traditionally, it rains every year before and after the fireworks in downtown St. Marys. The rain has become just as much of a tradition as the actual celebration.

Before my next thought, the rain came pouring down without many moments between each drop, making it impossible to dodge them. We started to run, jump, dance, and splash each other in the process. My hair, body, and attire were soaked once again. My hair was wild and free as the mascara started to run down my face. Jeremy, saw me with messed-up hair and without any makeup, and for the second time that day.

The rain stopped once we got back to our cars, and we decided to shoot off some of our own fireworks. Well, I say "we," but it was the guys who decided to do it. I thought, "These guys are crazy. Not only did Jeremy burn me, but now they are going to start a fire or something." I was freaked out. But they seemed to be pros in the fireworks area, so my nerves started to calm, and I was able to enjoy the show.

Once all of the fireworks were gone, we decided to hang out some more because the night was still young. The rain started back so Jeremy invited us to go to his house to watch movies. We were still soaked to the bone, so Jeremy gave all of us some dry clothes to change into. He gave me some Scooby-Doo pajama pants and a white long-sleeved shirt to wear. After that, we all quickly made ourselves comfortable.

Contemplation

Jeremy started the movie, and on our first night together, him and I curled up in each other's arms. I laid my head on his chest and started watching the movie and fell right asleep. Was I insane? With a perfect stranger, the first night we were together, I fell asleep. I felt a little better knowing that the man owned a pair of Scooby-Doo pajamas. How scary could he be? In addition, my sister was right beside me. But honestly, I had never felt more secure in my life. I felt safe in his arms; it was the weirdest feeling in the world to me.

I left that night with my sister, feeling like a million bucks. I knew that I had met the one that I was supposed to spend the rest of my life with. I didn't have to spend a lot of time with him. After one encounter, I was in love. I knew that it was God-ordained. All these thoughts continued to fill my mind, making me feel as if a weight had been lifted off my shoulders.

But once the weight started to lift, it was immediately followed by a series of crippling thoughts: "What if he doesn't like me back? What if he doesn't want to be around me because I am such a mess? What if he decides that I am not for him and chooses to run away from me because my imperfections are just too great?"

I was so scared that my raggedness was going to keep away the best thing that had ever walked into my life. I didn't know if I should be honest with him and share all my struggles with him, or hide all the garbage in my life and keep the smell to myself.

Reflection:

Has there ever been a time in your life that you thought, "this has to be God," but then doubt quickly settled in? Were you able to overcome the doubt?

Scripture Focus:

Matthew 14: 31, "Immediately Jesus reached out His hand, caught hold of him, and said to him, "You of little faith, why did you doubt?"

CHAPTER 10: THE PERFECT BODY

Nothing we see or hear is perfect.
But right there in the imperfection is perfect reality.
~Shunryu Suzuki

As I tried to decide what to do with all my garbage and wondered whether Jeremy was going to run for his life or not, the Lord took me back to my high school days at the radio station. I was like Scrooge going back to look at his life. I was there in my mind, standing in the back of the new Rock Bible Study building, finally out of the great battle of the mosquitoes, when it happened. I noticed that people kept racing by to hang out with their weekly friends, not uttering a single word to the boy in the back row.

Every week the same thing happened, and not many times did even a single person give him the time of day. I felt like I was watching a ghost who did not realize that he was dead so kept trying to talk to people, but all they did was walk right through him. I could not believe my eyes. Then I saw his mom close at his side, standing watch and protecting him in every way that she physically could to make sure that people did not bump into him or give him dirty looks.

His mom, his beautiful mom, had light-blonde hair that curled just like Curly Sue's. Her eyes were the bluest eyes that I had ever seen and as clear as a pool that you could see straight to the bottom of. But instead seeing the bottom of a pool, I could look into her eyes and see all the pain that she felt for her precious son. I could tell that her pain was deep, but at the same time, she was filled with love and pride for her son and his amazing heart. No matter how hard it may have been for her, she faithfully brought him to the Bible study every week. She did not just bring him on her own will, though. Caleb wanted to come and worship his maker with other believers, even if they ignored him in the process. He knew who saw him, and he knew that he mattered.

My heart ached for this young man. I remember the first time I went to speak to him. I leaned down to his chair on wheels to hear his response to my question. "Hi Caleb," I said. "My name is Tiffany. Did you enjoy the service tonight?" When he responded, it was hard to hear him or make out his words completely, so his sweet mom interpreted for me. But honestly, I did not have to hear his words or know the meaning behind them. His facial expression was enough for me. He had this huge smile on his face and a laugh so joyful that I could have listened to it for days and picked it out of any crowd. He was happy, and everyone around him knew it to be true.

In that moment, Jesus shined through Caleb brilliantly — through every part of him, even the broken parts. I desired to be a forever friend to him, and I wanted to know his secret. I did not understand how he could be so happy when his body was completely torn. I had to know how his joy was so secure.

An Unexpected Tragedy

I learned of Caleb's story just shortly after my first meeting with him, and it was intense. I found out that Caleb's body had been almost completely destroyed from a car accident when he was only seventeen years of age. His accident was so brutal that one of the stoplights in town had been installed as a direct result of his life-changing incident. His mother shared his story with me in detail, and I was shocked. My heart ached for him even more. Here is his story, in his mother's words:

The date was November 20, 1996, and it was like any other day, or so we thought. It started out as a normal school day and workday. Caleb's dad had come in from work after working the night shift. When he worked the night shift, Caleb got to drive to school the next morning. Caleb left for school and went to pick up his friend Andrew, like normal.

He left, and little did we know that when we saw him again, his life would be forever changed.

At 3:30 in the afternoon, I received a call from home, asking where Caleb was. I told my husband not to worry; there had been an accident at the intersection, but I never dreamed that Caleb was in the accident. I told my husband I hadn't heard from him and told him to call Caleb's friends' parents to see if Caleb had gone to see them. Then I got the call I was not expecting. My husband called to tell me that Caleb had been in an accident and that they had to Life Flight him to Jacksonville to the trauma unit of University Medical Center.

I left work, driving home to pick up my husband for us to travel to the hospital. When I arrived home, a policeman was at my door. It was then that I realized it was bad. I told the cop to let the doctors know of Caleb's allergies. Then I called to let my oldest son know about Caleb's accident. Thankfully, his girlfriend went and got him out of his college class. When we arrived at the hospital, we were approached by a cop who had been in the trauma unit where Caleb was. The cop told us Caleb was fighting for his life.

We waited, and it seemed like forever. Finally, one of the doctors came in to tell us the news: Caleb was seriously injured and must undergo a surgery that he might not survive. He had sustained a broken neck at C1–C2. He would have to have help breathing from now on. They told *us he had suffered the same kind of injury that Christopher Reeve had.*

We as a family sat and waited; it seemed like forever for his first surgery to be over. After we had waited three long hours, the doctor came to talk to us. All we got was bad news. Then, three days later the neurosurgeon came and took us into a private room, I knew it was bad news again. He told us Caleb needed emergency surgery on his neck. They took him to surgery, and we waited and prayed the whole time. It seemed like forever, getting occasional phone calls from surgery telling us how he was doing.

I thought to myself, "How will we survive if Caleb doesn't make it?" But I kept pushing that thought down; I couldn't allow myself to think like that. I knew God was in control, but I still worried about everyone involved: Caleb, his dad, his brother, his grandparents, and the rest of the family. Caleb had always kept us all in check, and we didn't want to think about the "what ifs." My heart was aching because my youngest son was fighting for his life, my oldest son was hurting for his brother, and I couldn't do a quick fix for either of them. My two sons were in pain. I felt helpless.

When the surgery was finally over, all I wanted was to go in and take care of Caleb. He was in ICU, and we were allowed to see him at any time as long as they weren't doing any procedures on him. We had good days and bad days. We had many friends praying for Caleb, as well as people we didn't even know. Still, it was hard to watch Caleb just lying there on the bed with no response coming from him. My heart was breaking, but I wanted to stay positive to help other family members.

I remember the second day when the doctor came in to talk to us. He told us he hadn't thought we would still be there because Caleb had only about a 10 percent chance of surviving. My father-in-law profoundly told him, "Doc, you do what you can, and God will do the rest." I repeated that over and over in my heart. I was not giving in to the fear, but you know the devil is going to be right there to try to convince you otherwise. Then we had a visit from a former pastor of ours, and he and his wife came and prayed for Caleb and told us not to let anyone with negative comments say anything around Caleb. So we began not to let negative comments be spoken around us or around Caleb. Oh yes, the devil tried, but we persevered.

On the third day that Caleb was in the hospital, the neurosurgeon came in to tell us the device holding Caleb's neck in place was not holding, and they needed to do immediate surgery, which would take eight to ten hours. We waited and waited for his surgery to be complete. Before the surgery, people from our church lined the hospital floor where Caleb would pass. We prayed for him as he passed by and prayed for him while he was in surgery. When the surgery was complete, he had a halo to hold his head in place.

On the twentieth day, we thought Caleb was coming out of his coma. He opened his eyes at his granny, who was making faces at him. The doctor came, and she thought it was a good sign. However, Caleb never woke up while we were there at the trauma unit. Next, we went to an acute-care hospital. They continued to work on Caleb there. Not much happened until one night in the ICU when Caleb heard a lady singing "When the Saints Go Marching In." He was laughing at her. We then realized that Caleb knew what was going on around him. We were there for almost three months.

Caleb had been the teen Sunday school teacher. He had dreams of being an architect, or so we had thought. Caleb was a senior in high school and had begun thinking about which college he wanted to attend. I couldn't believe that after all those dreams, my boy was so broken before me. We spent forty long days and nights in the trauma unit, never leaving Caleb alone at any time. We slept on the floor in the waiting room, going in throughout the night to see him. The hospital had gotten us a room at the Ronald McDonald House so we could take showers and rest a little. When some of the family would come to the hospital, my mother-in-law and I would go take a shower and a short nap, and then it was back to the hospital for the next round.

We eventually made our way to Jacksonville to Genesis Rehabilitation Hospital, where Caleb got his new beginning. He did all different kinds of therapy and

*even finished high school there and came home to grad-
uate with his class at Camden County High School. That
was an accomplishment in itself. His brother pushed him
across the stage to a standing-ovation crowd – his parents, grandparents, and other family members crying as
he crossed the stage.*

*Caleb came home after being gone six and one-half
months. We traveled back and forth for outpatient therapy
for months. When Caleb started to come around, he wanted
to start taking some college classes. He began taking classes
at World Harvest Bible College in Columbus, Ohio. He finished there, and on Mother's Day 2007, he graduated, with
interest in becoming a minister. Even though he is unable
to walk, he has already changed so many lives during the
time after his accident by simply being the Caleb that God
created him to be.*

Living In A Broken Society

When I met Caleb for the first time, it was easy to assume
that he was a sad person and hated the place he was in. Who
would want to be bound to a wheelchair for life? Now, I
am not saying that he never had his moments with anger
because of his accident, but at the Rock he never showed that
side. In the middle of worship, I would glance over and see
him raising his hands as high as he could, fighting his body's
desire to hold him back. I would hear him singing as loudly

as he could; even though it was difficult to make out his every word, I knew exactly what he was saying. He shouted his amen while each speaker spoke in order to encourage them in the Lord as much as possible. Caleb loved Jesus and he loved people, and no accident could hold him down from letting the world know that, because the power of Jesus resided in him. But was that enough for others?

Society's way of thinking is that if someone doesn't have the perfect body, hair, degree, background — the list is endless — the person does not belong. The person who is considered an outcast is shoved aside and replaced with the best of the best until society is functioning without a so-called kink or bend. To the ones who are the cream of the crop, life is good and functioning properly. Those left on the outside, however, wonder if they will ever get in and be able to use their gifts and talents to the best of their abilities. Unfortunately, if they are broken or full of blemishes, they are rarely accepted into the "in crowd" and are deserted to take over the leftovers, or even worse, the scraps on the floor.

In the church, these ideologies are not supposed to exist, but unfortunately, they do. The church is supposed to love the unlovable, accept the outcasts, and understand that God can use any person to give Him glory. But I have noticed that the church, just like society, ranks people by their looks and abilities instead of by the ability of God working within them and through them. If someone does not have a degree in ministry, wear the right clothes, say the right things, or have a family that never steps out of line, then they cannot be on the "dream team" at churches or in organizations, and be used to reach people for Christ. The church needs to realize that this is not how the family of God is expected to operate.

The church isn't called to look past people, the creations of God, and walk through them or look the other way. If a person is living and breathing, God has a plan for them and can be glorified in their body and life, for 1 Corinthians 12:4–6 explains: "There are diversities of gifts, but the same Spirit. There are differences of ministries, but the same Lord. And there are diversities of activities, but it is the same God who works all in all." First John 2:27 sheds further light on this truth: "But the anointing which you have received from Him abides in you, and you do not need that anyone teach you; but as the same anointing teaches you concerning all things, and is true, and is not a lie, and just as it has taught you, you will abide in Him."

A Modern Day Hero

Whenever I came in contact with Caleb during my many years at the station, I never once heard him complain about his body. He always used whatever energy he had left from the day to encourage others around him or me. He didn't have to have legs that could walk, arms that worked properly, or a mouth that could utter words clearly. He may have wanted that from time to time, and I am sure that Caleb's mom saw him shed many tears over the years. However, his desire and love for the Lord and others was what really mattered most to Caleb, because those things could go on forever, for eternity. He knew where his anointing came from. He knew that Jesus was sufficient, and even though his flesh and heart might fail, God was the strength of his heart and portion forever (see Psalm 73:26). He knew that even if his body were in full working order…he would still be a pile of dry, dead bones with out God…

> *He knew that even if his body were in full working order… he would still be a pile of dry, dead bones with out God…*

In Ezekiel 37:1–14, one of my favorite stories lives. It is an ideal picture of how much our bodies need God to operate. Of course, in Genesis 2:7, I am reminded that man was formed out of dust by the hand of God, and his lungs filled with air by His breath. In Genesis 3:19, I am reminded that man will return to dust someday. But in Ezekiel 37, the unthinkable happens.

Imagine a valley full of dry bones lying lifeless in the presence of a man named Ezekiel, upon whom the power of God rests. Can't get a picture of it? Think about the scene in *The Lion King* when Simba and Nala are walking through *the elephant graveyard*. God calls Ezekiel, through His Spirit, down to the valley to face these bones head-on and asks him in verse 3, "Son of man, can these bones live?" Ezekiel replies, "Lord God, only You know." God calls Ezekiel to prophesy to the bones and say to them: "Dry bones, hear the word of the Lord! This is what the Lord God says to these bones: I will cause breath to enter you, and you will live. I will put tendons on you, and cover your skin. I will put breath in you so that you come to life. Then you will know that I am Yahweh" (verses 4–6).

Then something never seen before and extremely difficult for the human mind to comprehend starts to happen right before his eyes. The bones that once lay lifeless before him, start to rattle and shake. I cannot imagine this sight. I am sure that if I had been standing before those bones, I would have run in the opposite direction from disgust and fear, even though I knew God's power existed in that moment. To see it so plainly in front of me would have been a frightening yet an exciting sight.

The bones clang and bang together at attention while the earth shakes beneath Ezekiel's feet from all the commotion, and then, verses 7–8 reveal: "So I prophesied as I had been commanded. While I was prophesying, there was a noise, a rattling sound, and the bones came together bone to bone. As I looked, tendons appeared on them, flesh grew, and skin covered them." Right after that, God commanded him to prophesy that breath would enter into their lungs, and after breath from the four winds entered their bodies, "they came to life and stood on their feet, a vast army" (Ezekiel 37:10).

When I read this story, so much comes to mind. I wonder how the place smelled; those bones had been lying there for a long time. I wonder if Ezekiel was the least bit scared or if he was completely confident in God. Then I think about the bones. I wonder, were the bones perfect when they were lying in the deep valley below? No, they were not. They were broken, tattered, worn, and lifeless without the mighty power of God in them. My friend Caleb understood these truths and still does today. He is fully aware

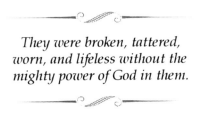

They were broken, tattered, worn, and lifeless without the mighty power of God in them.

that God is the giver of life. He knows that the "perfect" bodies that we think we will have forever are lifeless without God to breathe life into them and give them purpose.

To others, Caleb's body may be tattered, worn, and broken because of an unforgiving accident, but the Spirit of Jesus is in him. He is such an amazing person and continues to amaze me daily. As of now, he may not be able to preach behind a pulpit, lead worship, or help young children, but he is a part of the body of Christ just as much as anybody else, and he doesn't let his body keep him down. Honestly, Caleb ministers more to me than anyone else does in my life; he inspires me in so many ways…he is my modern day hero. He continues to take classes, pray for people, and work towards his goal of becoming a preacher one day, even if he needs help to do it. He allows Jesus to work in and through his brokenness.

We pray that Caleb will walk again one day, but even if he doesn't, Caleb has chosen to be thankful for every day that he is given from the Lord. He does not need to have the greatest body in order to live for Jesus every chance he gets. He knows that this life is temporary, and that no matter how shattered he may seem to everyone else, Jesus loves him. He knows that through Jesus' power within him, he can be used. Most importantly of all, Caleb knows that Jesus doesn't run away from the mess — He runs to it with all His might.

Reflection:

Have you ever met or known someone like Caleb who was faced with an unexpected situation, such as an accident or a newfound disease, that caused him or her to be limited in some way? Did they maintain their spiritual integrity like Caleb did? How inspiring was their ability to rely on God even through their struggles.

Scripture Focus:

Romans 8: 28, "We know that all things work together for the good of those who love God: those who are called according to His purpose."

Philippians 4: 12-13, "I know both how to have a little, and I know how to have a lot. In any and all circumstances I have learned the secret of being content — whether well fed or hungry, whether in abundance or in need. I am able to do all things through Him who strengthens me.

CHAPTER 11: THE HEART OF JESUS

We love because He first loved us.

~1 John 4:19

There was a young man who grew up with a rich father. The father gave him everything that he could possibly want. His daily bread was accounted for, and so was his future through his inheritance. However, the young man refused to appreciate any of it. Nothing that his father gave him was good enough. He wanted to be free from the prison that he thought he was in. I say "thought" because really, it was a prison he had created himself. He was trapped by his own desired reality in his own mind, and tired of being controlled by others telling him how to live his life. He wanted to be independent instead of being told what to do all the time. So he took matters into his own hands and asked his father for his inheritance.

Instead of putting his inheritance to good use, he depleted his entire estate on foolish living. The son was at the end of his rope after he lost everything — including his pride. One day he found himself surrounded by this awful smell that was unbearable, but he was so hungry that none of it mattered. He heard the sound of animals right beside him as he shoved as much food into his mouth as he possibly could, not caring how much of it was smashed upon his face. He looked to his left . . . he looked to his right . . . and saw pigs beside him.

He was eating with his new best friends — pigs. The smell engulfed his nostrils once again, and finally, reality hit him smack in the face. He realized that he had never been in this place before. He had hit the lowest point in his life. He missed his life back home. He missed his father, and he wanted to return to him. He knew that even his father's slaves lived better than he was living right in that moment. But what would he say to his father? Would his father accept him and take him back, even with the horrible mistakes he had made?

The boy was determined to go home and ask his father to forgive him for the money he had wasted and for the way that he had acted, but he was extremely scared to approach him. He knew he had messed everything up — including blowing his inheritance. The young man just knew that his father would never be able to forgive him for his mistakes. Regardless of his thoughts, he made the choice to return home to be with his family and face his punishment. He said to himself, "Even if I live like a slave in my father's court, I will be better off than I am now."

As he made the journey home, he put together the pieces in his mind of how he was going to ask his father to accept him back into the family. Butterflies filled his stomach as the words overflowed in his mind of all that he wanted to say. His body rattled as each step was taken closer and closer to home. He was filthy from his long journey home and from being on his knees living like the pigs. "There is no way that my father will ever forgive me," he believed to himself as he saw in the distance a mirage of his father walking towards him.

Before another thought could cross his tired mind, he realized that it wasn't a mirage. His father, his loving father, was coming to greet him. And he wasn't just walking to greet him—*he was running*. His father was running toward him with

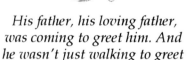

His father, his loving father, was coming to greet him. And he wasn't just walking to greet him – he was running.

every ounce of strength that he had stored in his body in the hope that this exact moment would come to pass, that his son would decide to return home.

The son thought for sure that his father would stop before he got to him, once he saw how much of a mess he was. But once his father was an arm's length away from his son, the unthinkable happened. He grabbed his son as quickly as he could, threw his arms around his neck, and kissed him. The son was embarrassed and voiced, "'Father, I have sinned against heaven and in your sight. I'm no longer worthy to be called your son" (Luke 15:21).

"But the father told his slaves, 'Quick! Bring out the best robe and put it on him; put a ring on his finger and sandals on his feet. Then bring the fattened calf and slaughter it, and let's celebrate with a feast, because this son of mine was dead and is alive again; he was lost and is found!' So they began to celebrate" (Luke 15: 22-24). His father did not care how much of a mess his son was in; he was just glad that his son had finally returned home. His son didn't have to do anything to win his father's love. His father just loved him and accepted him where he was in life. He was fully broken—physically, mentally, emotionally, and financially—with the smell of pigs on him. His father did not care. He immediately pushed all those things aside and called for a celebration—his son was home!

The Great Wall

Just like this young man, I could not see or believe that Jesus was running towards me with all His might. Because of all that I had gone through, I forgot the heart of Jesus. I was blinded by my own self-condemnation. The closer He ran towards me, the farther I moved from Him. I wanted to keep my distance and turn my face away from His because I felt like I had failed Him.

I had quit school—a Christian school, nonetheless—and destroyed my body in more ways than one. I wondered how in the world He could use someone so dismembered. I longed to be like the young man in the parable and Caleb; to finally be able to embrace the Savior with all of my junk, to see God as a loving God, and His Son for who He truly is, a loving Savior who runs towards the mess and accepts people where they are in life. Sadly, I couldn't. I just kept running farther away. How could He fully accept me?

When I tried to spend time with Him, there was this great wall between us. The wall was nothing that He had done; I had built it all on my own. However, I blamed Him for its presence, all the while placing a new brick each day to increase its height. The top of the wall eventually grew beyond my reach, and I was in the mud with the pigs, wasting my life. I would look up from my pit with my neck stretched all the way back to my shoulders, hoping to see its end in sight, but it was too tall. I begged Jesus to bring me out of the pit, but I was too stubborn to give up my way of my life. I thought that I could fool Him and others by staying in the pit and covering up my smell with religious acts, pretending like everything was okay.

Even though I knew what a true loving relationship with the Lord looked like, my eyes were covered with the devil's snakeskin lies. All I saw were the things I could try to do in order to make Jesus accept me and love me. I didn't want to be vulnerable and let Jesus in to fix me — to accept me where I was, break the walls down, pull me out of the pit, and lovingly clean the mud off me. I wanted to fix myself.

Stuck

I was overcomplicating the heart of Christianity far too much. I thought to myself that if I could just sing more worship songs, read and memorize more Scripture, pray and help more at the church, then I would be covered and Jesus would accept me with open arms. I knew that all these things were beneficial to me and other people in the kingdom of God, but I also knew that they were not the most important things. Unfortunately, all too often they were my main focus.

I felt like I was constantly tripping up in my relationship with Jesus because of simple things that did not matter much to Him, such as accidentally sleeping in so that my Bible time was missed in the morning or, even worse, shamefully missed sometimes for the entire day. I thought that keeping tasks was what moved God.

I thought that God was mad at me or that He was going to send down blazing fire because I was not perfect all the

I thought that God was mad at me or that He was going to send down blazing fire because I was not perfect all the time.

time. I argued, "I mean, that is how He did things in the Old Testament, right?" My mind was warped, and I had forgotten all the things I had learned at such an early age about Jesus and His endless love for me. Jesus needed to get through to me, but I was not making it easy for Him. The walls were still up, and blinders were still over my eyes. I was stuck.

Jesus was having such a hard time getting through to me, so He decided to use Jeremy. But even then, I often pondered, "If I am not perfect enough for Jesus to accept me, then how in the world is Jeremy going to accept me?" I couldn't tell Jeremy the truth. I couldn't tell him that I was a recovering anorexic and a newfound bulimic. I couldn't reveal to him that I had quit school because of my issues and that I had failed God miserably. All these things would keep him away from me, for sure. I reeked of garbage but did my best to cover it up with the cheap perfume of lies.

The Big Reveal

After our first night together, Jeremy and I stayed in touch as much as we could. He was in the navy and had a lot of demands. I was three hours away from him because I was still living with my dad and stepmom, Marie. We would talk on the phone all the time and see each other whenever we could. In the beginning, when we were around each other, I did my best to hold it together for both Jesus and Jeremy.

But after a while, I let things go. We were on the phone one night and like vomit coming forth from a sickness, I couldn't swallow it down any longer; especially since Jeremy was due to go out to sea soon. I had to tell him the truth. Tears started to fill my eyes as I tried to think of the best words to use. Truthfully, there were no right words to unload the truckload of stuff that I had. I was so scared to tell him the truth. Pain filled my stomach as the words came forth and filled his mind with doubt—so I thought.

"Jeremy, I am a mess. I come from a broken home. Every relationship I have had has failed. I had to quit school because I wasn't strong enough to fight off anorexia by myself. Now I am dealing with bulimia. I have been seeing a counselor for about two months now, but I am thinking of quitting that too because I have failed at that as well. I understand if you do not want to be with me anymore or talk to me anymore."

Words cannot express how thankful I was to hear his returned words: "Tiffany, it is okay. We are all broken, imperfect, but it's your imperfections that make you beautiful." I could not believe the words that I had heard. A huge weight was lifted off my shoulders in that moment. As soon as I decided to let everything go and those words came out of Jeremy's mouth, the smell began to disappear, the wall started to tumble, and the mud started to wash from my face. Through Jeremy, thankfully, I was reminded of the real heart of Jesus.

The Jesus People Forget About

Jesus came to show the world a new, different way from the norm. He came to reveal the heart of the Father, which is to love. Jesus voiced the greatest commandment in Matthew 22:36–40:

> "Teacher, which is the greatest commandment in the Law?"
>
> Jesus replied: "'Love the Lord your God with all your heart and with all your soul and with all your mind.' This is the first and greatest commandment. And the second is like it: 'Love your neighbor as yourself.' All the Law and the Prophets hang on these two commandments."

He said that the two most important things in life are to love God and to love people.

Jeremy reminded me of my favorite thing about Jesus: He does not just say empty words, but He puts words into action. He did everything that He could during His short time on the earth and, more importantly, His short time in ministry to show the love of God to others. Jesus did this by always going out of His way for others even when it was hard for Him.

Matthew 14:14, is a huge testimony to this fact, and it states, "When Jesus landed and saw a large crowd, he had compassion on them and healed their sick." In this passage, I see a Jesus who cared in the midst of His own pain. In the beginning of Matthew 14, something tragic happened to one of Jesus' closest friends in ministry, John the Baptist. Shortly after the disciples told Him about John's death, He went to pull away to take a moment to Himself. Matthew 14:13 says, "When Jesus heard what had happened, he withdrew by boat privately to a solitary place. Hearing of this, the crowds followed him on foot from the towns."

I know that this must have been devastating for Jesus to go through. I know all too well what it is like to lose a friend or someone very close to my heart. In those moments, all I wanted to do was pause my life for a while so that I could cope with everything in my own way and in my own time. I too wanted to pull away and curl up in a hole until the aching stopped. In Matthew 14, the Son of Man, the Son of God, was devastated because of the loss of a friend. He strategically pulled away so that He could cope. The first thing that happened, however, was that a large crowd turned to Him for help.

I know that if I were in that situation, I would not want to see anyone at that time, especially a huge crowd of people needing my help. I would find a new place to hide so the crowd couldn't find me, playing the ultimate game of hide-and-seek. But Jesus didn't respond the way I would. Instead of turning the people away and saying, "I do not have time for this right now; I have my own problems," He chose to respond with all the love in His heart. He went to them.

When Jesus saw the large crowd, He was moved with compassion and went to help them: "He had compassion on them" (Matthew 14:14). Some translations even say that Jesus was *moved* with compassion. In other words, Jesus went towards the mess. Moreover, He did not just go towards a little mess; He went towards a *big* mess and met them where they were. He healed them, and even more so, He fed them.

"As evening approached, the disciples came to him and said, 'This is a remote place, and it's already getting late. Send the crowds away, so they can go to the villages and buy themselves some food'" (Matthew 14:15). Jesus replied in verse 16, "They do not need to go away. You give them something to eat."

Most people know the rest of the story. The disciples argued with Jesus, saying that they had only five loaves and two fishes. There was no way that was going to feed the vast number of people sitting before them. Jesus took the fish, gave thanks, and broke the loaves. The disciples began to pass out the food, and to their surprise, the numbers multiplied as the people kept coming forth. The amount of food was enough to make everyone present "belly-aching" satisfied. Verse 21 reveals the number of people who were present: "The number of those who ate was about five thousand men, besides women and children."

When I look at verse 21, I cannot believe those numbers. The Bible tells only the number of men. The truth is, no one will ever know the actual number of women and children who were there that day; it could have been double or even triple the number of men. The main thing that blows my mind is not just the fact that Jesus fed all these people, but that He took the time to bring healing to those who needed it, no matter how big or small the need was.

When Jeremy decided to accept me the way I was and to love me anyway, I was reminded that Jesus did not see the crowd and run in the opposite direction. Jesus decided to continue towards the hurt, the tattered, and the worn. He saw the needy and wanted to help them. He saw me and wanted to help me. He wanted to completely tear down the wall that I had built between us. He wanted to take me out of the pit and clean me up for good, but it would be a while before I would let that happen.

Reflection:

How does it make you feel to be reminded of the heart of Jesus; That He continues towards the tattered, the worn, and the messy? Do you see yourself as a mess? If you do, does it lift off a heavy weight knowing that Jesus runs to the mess and not away from it? Does it give you a new sense of freedom that this is the true heart of Jesus?

Scripture Focus:

Matthew 14: 13-14, "When Jesus heard about it, He withdrew from there by boat to a remote place to be alone. When the crowds heard this, they followed Him on foot from the towns. As He stepped ashore, He saw a huge crowd, felt compassion for them, and healed their sick.

CHAPTER 12: I'M SO BUSY

Beware the barrenness of a busy life.

~Socrates

There comes a time in every girl's life when a huge paradigm shift from girl to woman takes place. Most of the time, it's not something that can be planned for — it just happens. One day, girls care about playing dress up or playing with dolls, but then the next day, boys become the center of attention. For me, I wasn't into playing dress up or with dolls all that much; I cared more about getting dirty in the mud and playing sports. But once I hit the paradigm shift, I changed from caring about playing sports with guys to wanting to date them. I dated a few guys in high school, but they did not capture my attention like the one boy, or should I say, the man, who came into my life.

I remember many times before, after the shift started to take place, I would ask my mom the same question, begging for a better answer than she would give me time and time again. I would ask, "Mom, when will I know when I find the right *one*?"

"Tiffany, you just know, sweetie. No one can ever really explain it to you, but when God shows you the right man to be in your life, trust me — you will know who 'the one' is."

I hated the answer I got from her, which often ended with me rolling my eyes and shouting out an "ugh" as I walked away, stomping my feet harder and harder on the ground, banging out all my frustrations. "Ha, the *one*," I would think. Honestly, it was an impossible but thought-provoking concept. I often convinced myself that it would never happen because finding "the one" was like trying to find the real Waldo in a sea of striped-wearing imposters. I was doomed.

Then, all of a sudden like a curveball to the face, it happened — *he* happened. Jeremy walked into my life, and everything changed. When I found him, I knew that he was "the one." I felt like I had found the perfect pair of shoes to wear to the prom but was worried they might break, but on a much greater scale, of course. The one thing that I feared I would never find became the main thing I feared to lose.

I started to question how we would last. "I come from a broken home. Relationships don't last. There is absolutely no way that Jeremy and I will make it long at all," I thought. But I was so excited that he was in my life, that instead of letting those kind of thoughts take over my life, I tried my hardest to shove them deep within my soul. Jeremy and I were together, and I was the happiest I had been in the longest time. I decided to hold on and do my best to enjoy the ride in spite of the "negative Nancys" in my mind.

"The One" Does Exist

In the onset, when we met on the Fourth of July, we just clicked; something switched on in both of us. We just knew that we were meant to be. Two weeks after that, we were discussing the type of ring a wife would like. Crazy, I know, but that was the least of it. Things got increasingly strange with each passing moment.

Jeremy was in the Navy on submarines, which meant that he had to leave for three to four months at a time. Honestly, it wasn't a huge deal at first that he had to leave, since I lived with my dad three hours away and we were used to having some distance between us. We rarely had conversations face-to-face. Most of them were over the phone.

When he was gone for the first time, I e-mailed him almost every day. I wasn't trying to be super obsessive; I just felt better when I did. Ever since he had told me that he loved me because of my imperfections, I felt so free to share my days, let go, and make sure he knew that I was thinking of him often. I was in love, and everyone around me knew it to be true. Even those who weren't around me knew that Jeremy and I were in love.

Before he left on his first sea excursion away from me, he told me that I should call his family sometime, and he gave me their phone number. I was so nervous the first time that I called. I thought, "Man, his family is really going to think that I am extremely unhinged." I went against my better judgment and called them anyway. The first time I called, I talked to his dad for forty-five minutes. Apparently, that was unheard of because his dad didn't talk on the phone much. However, looking back, I don't recall that he did; I talked his ear off. I was so nervous that all I could do was fill the awkward silence with my noise, my incoherent babbling.

I was so lost without Jeremy on the solid ground, but e-mailing, talking to his family, and love from my family made it tolerable. I could not wait to have him in my arms again. I did all that I knew to do to pass the time as quickly as possible. I would go to school, do my homework, pick up extra shifts at the YMCA that I was working at, and exercise. I exercised a lot in order to keep to the size that I desired, but mostly I did it to work off the excessive amount of nervous energy that I had acquired. Days were just not the same without hearing his voice through the phone. Mostly, my days were monotonous, until one glorious day . . .

Time stood still as I fought to tame the tigers in my stomach as I nervously waited for my sailor to return to me. I couldn't believe that three months had passed — it felt like an eternity. We hadn't even gone on a real date yet. I couldn't believe that I felt so strongly about Jeremy after only a short time.

I saw the boat near the shore, and I waited as patiently as I could for Jeremy to show his face above the surface of the sea. Seagulls flew overhead, singing a song of victory "we had made it." The wind swept by vigorously, carrying off my aching memories of the past three months without him.

Finally, it was his time to come off the boat. When I saw his face, I hardly recognized him at all. His face was painted with pale skin and dark circles all the way down to his cheek-bones. I tried my best to contain my excitement. I am sure that I was smiling from ear to ear. However, when I hugged him, I was afraid to break him — not because of my thrill to see him again, but because he looked so much smaller than before. He had endured months of eating less and denying himself the powdered milk of "deliciousness" upon his home made of steel.

He was back in my arms, and I wanted to stay in that moment forever. If I close my eyes today, I can still smell the salty air, hear the seagulls above, and feel his newly revealed ribs in the hug of my arms. The moment was so beautiful, regardless of my concern for his health at the time — the man needed a steak and potatoes pronto! As much as I wanted the moment to last, it went by far too quickly, and so did every other moment that followed.

The Fast Lane

Jeremy and I met in July 2005. He went out to sea from the end of July all the way until the end of October. After he returned, he started telling me that I should move in with him. I said, "Well, that requires a few things: (1) your own house and (2) a ring." Things didn't take long, because not too long after that, he had his own place and asked me to marry him — with an amazing ring, I might add — in December 2005. Needless to say, I moved back to my hometown, staying with some friends and preparing for a wedding faster than you can say, "Here comes the bride." We were married in April 2006 and settled into our new home after our honeymoon in Jamaica. I once again landed my dream job back at the radio station. Life was perfect . . . mostly.

The part that stunk, as the nastiest-smelling skunk in the world, was being a newlywed and having to say good-bye every couple of months to the man of my dreams. Plus, I still sometimes dealt with anorexia and bulimic tendencies, although those were few and far between. I was thankful the bouts were becoming less frequent, but it was still difficult to go through.

I hated saying good-bye. I also hated trying to be super perky on the air at the station when on the inside I felt incomplete and dead, longing for my husband. Most of the time, I just wanted to bury my head in a pillow and sleep. "Ahhhh, sleep will make it go by more quickly," I thought, because when we were dating, being busy hadn't helped at all. The days dragged on and on.

Regrettably, I do wish that at the time I had focused on and taken in the good that was in front of my face as plain as day. Sadly, fog filled most of my days, but underneath it all, there was good. The station was such an amazing place to be at daily; ministering to others over the air was so much fun and so fulfilling. But I was too caught up in the moment, and all I wanted was my husband. At the time, there wasn't much else that could satisfy. I wished that life would speed up even more, so that he wouldn't have to go out to sea any more.

Luckily, eventually I got my wish and I did not have to deal with him leaving me anymore. Once again, in the blink of an eye, years passed and all the good and the bad were behind us. Jeremy received orders to Charleston, South Carolina.I was so thankful to leave in the past the bad of him leaving all the time, because now I was able to see him daily. That was a dream come true.

However, I wasn't ready to leave the station behind for the second time in my life. Truthfully, when it came down to it, I wasn't ready for the real world as it truly was—out of the safety nest of my hometown, where everyone loved me and I had one of the coolest jobs in the entire world. The Navy packed our bags for the first time as a married couple, and we headed to the great unknown.

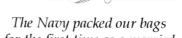

The Navy packed our bags for the first time as a married couple, and we headed to the great unknown.

I quickly tried to get used to our new home in Charleston. I did my best to blend into the larger city. I got a job right away at a gym. I was a salesperson. I had to sell memberships. I was thankful for my base pay of five hundred dollars every two weeks because I was terrible at making sales. I would say things like, "Aw, you can't afford it. That's okay. You can run laps around your neighborhood for free and get the same results." Other sales personnel were pushy or made people feel uncomfortable or terrible for the way they looked. I just could not say things like, "Uh, you are overweight, and you cannot afford not to buy a membership, even if it means you can't afford a payment. Find a way!"

People that I worked with could tell that I wasn't that great at selling memberships, so they mentioned personal training to me. The head of personal training eventually asked if I wanted to train instead because he had seen the way that I worked out. He promised that he would pay me my base pay for doing intakes (measurements of women) for two weeks during a new program they were starting at the gym. After that was over, then I could train.

Well, I was there all day and all evening for two straight weeks, and I never saw a penny of that money. I had never met people who were so dishonest. Needless to say, my time there was stressful and short-lived. I cried almost every day when I got home from work because the personal-training head was so rude. I was relieved when I did eventually get my personal-training certificate and was able to move on to the YMCA once again.

I continued to train there, and life sped up even faster for Jeremy and me. While working at the Y, a miracle happened. After about a year of trying, we found out that I was pregnant with our first child. I was in total denial. I took probably five tests after the initial test. I spread them out for a week. I just couldn't believe that I was going to be a mom. Furthermore, the world was too awful to bring a child into the likes of it. "What did we do?" I anxiously pondered.

"Germophobe"

I was scared. I wondered how I would protect something so precious to me and keep him safe from harm. I couldn't believe that God trusted me to care for another human being. Slowly but surely, I turned into the "crazy mom" — a psycho-crazy, "germophobe," overprotective mom. Everything had to be clean — *all the time*. If things weren't in perfect order, I could feel the chaos all around me. I could feel the germs growing and taunting me

> *Slowly but surely, I turned into the "crazy mom" – the psycho-crazy, "germophobe," overprotective mom. Everything had to be clean – all the time.*

because no matter how much I cleaned, they would always exist. I was even frightened to take our new baby anywhere for fear of him getting sick. I was inside our home all the time — my prison cell.

Our baby turned two, we had our second child closely after, and my fears grew along with our family. Jesus was shouting to me from the rooftop, "Spend time with Me. I will give you rest!" But I couldn't stop cleaning the house, keeping babies away from germs, and finishing up my "actual" online college degree that I started, in the comfort of my own home, away from society and sickness. I thought that I was close to my family and the heart of Jesus, but I was anything but close. I had finally done it: I was too busy for anything in life that really mattered. I had become Martha.

In the Bible, Martha scrambled to clean the house in order to serve Jesus while "selfish" Mary sat at His feet to listen to all that He had to say. Martha's anger burned within, and she started to clang her dishes together to try to get someone's attention, but everyone ignored her noise. She finally got angry enough to speak her frustration to Jesus. In Luke 10:40, she said, "Lord, don't You care that my sister has left me to serve alone? So tell her to give me a hand." The Lord answered her in verse 41: "Martha, Martha, you are upset about many things, but one thing is necessary. Mary has made the right choice, and it will not be taken away from her."

I thought for sure that I was close to Jesus and all those around me, but I wasn't. I did all that I could do in order to keep busy instead of focusing on all the issues I had going on inside, that I had buried deep within and carried with me for years. I thought that if I stayed busy, I wouldn't have to sit quietly at Jesus' feet to learn just how messed up I really was. He wanted to help me, to share intimate time with me like He did with Mary. But I had better things to do. I finally became what I feared the most: so busy controlling my "put together life" life that I wasn't living life at all.

Reflection:

Have you ever made your life busy on purpose in order to ignore a problem or problems that you knew was there? Have you made yourself busy in order to feel accomplished or feel of worth? Have you been so busy to the point of pushing away the One that you knew you needed the most or the one thing you knew you needed to be doing?

Scripture Focus:

Psalm 46: 10, "Stop your fighting--and know that I am God, exalted among the nations, exalted on the earth."

Matthew 11: 28, "Come to Me, all of you who are weary and burdened, and I will give you rest."

PART 4
RUNNING MASCARA

Tears run down her face, mascara stains her cheeks,
slowly she's fading, falling. Realizing, she whispers it to
herself, "I can't do this anymore."

~Author unknown

This is where it all begins; everything starts here, today.

~David Nicholls

One Day

CHAPTER 13: BEHIND ENEMY LINES

*You are of your father the Devil, and you want
to carry out your father's desires.
He was a murderer from the beginning and
has not stood in the truth,
because there is no truth in him.
When he tells a lie, he speaks from his own nature,
because he is a liar and the father of liars.*

~John 8: 44

The sun danced in the distance as it made its way to hide its face for the night. My children spun in circles as their laughter filled the air. Normally, this would have been my favorite moment of the day to join in with, to be a part of, to add my laughter to God's beautiful symphony. Instead, I sat paralyzed with fear, unable to move in any direction. When I did decide to move, I felt like a snail inching its belly across uneven ground.

My thoughts rolled in like storm clouds coming to destroy the lovely moment: "How did I become so broken?

How did I get this far? Will I ever be the same again?" I hated this place in my mind. My family, my beautiful family, was full of life, and I felt like I was being the "fun sucker." I thought I was the one holding us back from complete joy. Even though I knew that my God, my Savior, had won the victory over my life, I felt defeated by the enemy with every inch I moved. The enemy was fighting for my affection while trapping my every waking thought and any attempt at forward motion.

The girl I once was would spin wild and free without a care in the world. For fun, she would lie flat on her back and pick out shapes, like a fluffy Mickey Mouse or jumping dolphins, in the clouds above. But in the moment before me, as my world spun violently out of control, with weakened knees I fell and finally hit rock bottom. The only thing I could see in the clouds above was imperfect shapes laughing at me because I would never measure up. My lifelong pursuit for perfection had finally brought me to a place I despised — I was behind enemy lines.

I know that it didn't happen overnight. I know that it started when I was young and free. Even then, the enemy studied me and jotted down notes on how I would react to situations: the things I would say, the way I would act, or how I would sometimes look at others and wish I were someone else. Those petty things that no one else looked at, he noticed. To him, nothing was miniscule, and he used everything as perfect ammo to shoot holes into my comfortable life. His main weapon of choice was fear.

I know it's a common trap that he chooses, but since it happened slowly over time, like a frog in boiling water, I never saw it coming. He chose this weapon for me for the same reason he chooses it for most Christians. He wants us to be paralyzed in fear; he wants us to feel alone, away from people, so that he can slowly chip away at us. Most of all, he wants us to question God's character and hopes that anger fills our hearts towards Him.

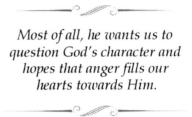

Most of all, he wants us to question God's character and hopes that anger fills our hearts towards Him.

Looking back, I can see that the small fears I had as a child, such as a fear of thunderstorms, the dark, and frogs, grew to so much more as I got older and faced new situations. After the birth of our second child, I stepped on a series of land mine the enemy had strategically placed in my path long before. All my fears, along with my comfortable life, blew up in my face. For starters, my husband, after completing ten years in the Navy prayerfully decided to take a leap of faith and leave the military. Our family decision meant moving a two-and-a-half-year-old toddler and a six-weeks-old baby. All the while, I was still recovering from giving birth. We were nervous because we did not know where my husband's job would take us, or even if he would find a job.

The Lord really looked after us in a big way during this time. Just one month prior to getting out of the Navy, my husband landed a job at a nuclear power plant. We were so thankful and relieved. The job was perfect, with great benefits. We were able to find suitable renters for our home after interviewing only two candidates. The military packed our bags for the last time, and we were on our way to a new, "safe" adventure. We were extremely blessed. Then it happened — the bottom fell out beneath us. Unfortunately, we were unable to latch onto anything while falling fast on our way to the hardest place we had ever been as a married couple.

Sneaky Devil

Our nauseating journey started two weeks after we moved. We were just getting settled in our new home and making a new normal outside of the military lifestyle. We had already unpacked all our boxes, which was a first for us. Since we had moved a couple of times with the military, there always seemed to be those few boxes we never unpacked because we thought, "What's the point, if we are just going to have to pack it up again in three years?" But this time we were pretty much settled.

The only thing that we did not fully unpack, believe it or not, was our van, our amazing Volkswagen van. I loved that thing. The van was silver-blue and had leather seating, heated seats, and a great stereo system — not to mention that it had about a thousand dollars' worth of stuff in the back, including our double jogging stroller. I felt like a supermom with that vehicle. We left it alone, though, because we figured we would finish the inside of the house first.

We finished putting things in their places while our youngest took a nap and our oldest played near us while pretending to be his favorite Disney character in an empty cardboard box. Storms started to roll in, and the wind blew between the newly constructed walls of our beautiful Georgia home. Through the windows came whistling sounds that filled the air around us. In the midst of the storm, however, there was peace. We were a family of four with a husband and a daddy who didn't have to leave anymore. There were two boys in the midst who filled our hearts with joy, and life was great. But as soon as peace filled every inch of our new life, we quickly realized that we were just in the eye of the storm.

One morning when my husband went out for work, he was shocked to find that our van was gone. We had moved our children into a supposedly safe neighborhood. As a new mother of two in a new area, I was scared. After that incident, I immediately started to question the safety of our new home. I couldn't help but think, "Where in the world did we move our family?" The fears began to set in deep — land mine number one: fearing the area.

Shortly after things had begun to calm down and we got a new vehicle, I ended up having to go to doctor appointment after doctor appointment because of some issues I was having after the birth of my second child. I was in and out of the hospital for the entire next year, in and out of pain, once again all alone and away from family. For the entire first year after my second child was born, we spent most of our days inside away from the sun and watched movies.

Some would probably say that I was depressed, but at that moment in my life, I denied any and all accounts. I was just in pain, and that was all there was to it. Finally, after a year of struggling with small procedures, I found out that I needed to have actual surgery because I was still having trouble healing completely.

The day before surgery, a person rear-ended our new van while the kids were with me. Thankfully, it was not too bad, and I was still able to have the surgery. The surgery happened, and the day after surgery, I experienced one of the most frightening things ever that I would never wish upon anyone. I had been taking some medicine that the doctor insisted I take, but to my surprise, I was allergic to it. After a day of taking this medicine, major stuff went down. I was eating dinner calmly when I took another dose. My airways started to close, my breathing got shallow, and I was shaking all over. My husband called the ambulance, and my poor kids had to watch it all.

Luckily, it wasn't as severe as what it could have been, but for me it was a life- threatening experience, and it changed me tremendously. Land mine number two: I started to fear my well-being, my health and my children's health, and medicine and how it could affect those close to me. I had never before thought about allergic reactions, but turned into something I thought about literally every second of the day. In spite of everything, I tried my best to keep moving forward.

After another six months, I finally healed completely in my body, and I felt more like myself. However, my mind still wasn't completely healed. Instead of focusing too much attention on that, I decided that being in the house as much as we were had to stop. I began to steer my attention to working out again. I was able to work out like I used to in high school. I felt great. I began to pour into my body and take care of it as much as I could, and I began getting the kids out more too. Of course, that led to joining a gym and attending as much as I could.

One day when I was at the gym, a man who I at first thought was a woman came up to me and shook my hand. "Hi, my name is Melody," he said.

"Okay, it has to be a woman. Her name is Melody," I thought to myself, doubting my every thought. As he/she continued having a conversation with me, she explained that she made a lot of money and wanted to give me a scholarship for my student loans. I thought, "Did I just meet an angel?"

I had lots of student loans from my online business degree. I was a stay-at-home mom who could not work, and I wanted to have this situation to be true. I wanted to be able to help my husband and not be a financial burden on our family. Listening as she explained further, I told her it would be amazing if she could do that for me. She said it was something that she did all the time. She told me to come back the next day to pick up the check. I immediately called my husband as soon as I got to the car and said, "I encountered either an angel of the Lord or a really creepy person."

I was either smart or stupid; most people reading this might feel as if a horror movie is flashing and might be thinking, "Please tell me you did not go back to the gym the next day!" Unfortunately, yes, I decided to go back to the gym the next day. When I showed up the next day, I started my workout with my usual three-mile run on the upstairs track. Every single time I got to the ledge, I would look down to the main floor, hoping to see this person. Hey, this person was going to give me money for college; I was not going to pass on the opportunity. Every time I passed by, I never saw her/him. "Lies, all lies!" I thought.

But as soon as I stopped running, went downstairs, and started lifting weights, Melody showed up. "Hey, Tiffany, it's me. Listen, I meant to bring the check to you today, but I forgot. But I decided that I wanted to give you a pedicure." Melody proceeded to tell me the name of the nail place and said that when I went to the nail place, the check for school would be waiting there. Trust me — I was not dumb enough to do that, but honestly, I was so shocked that I didn't even think, "Run — go tell someone."

I was literally stopped dead in my tracks like a frightened deer in the headlights. Once I regained my vision, I responded, "Um, no thank you. I don't think my husband would approve of that."

Melody walked away and started living heavy weights. A person called out and said, "Hey, Jim."

"Jim?" I wondered. I had known that this girl was a guy! I was terrified. Before I could get off of my weight bench Melody — I mean, Jim — came back over and said, "So, your name is Tiffany, and you have brown hair and green eyes" and proceeded to walk away. This person knew my name and what I looked like.

At this point, I still didn't think to go tell someone. The only thing I was thinking about was my children. I had to get my children out of there. Then the thought occurred to me that this person could have followed me home the day before. I was about to lose it. I told my husband everything, and then that night, following the counsel of my mom, I filed a police report and gave a description of the man. Needless to say, I quit going to that gym and, for the most part, avoided going anywhere. I was so scared that he was going to show up out of nowhere or, even worse, show up at my home. I was like the worst case of a momma bear you have ever seen. I even remember answering the door with a knife once.

But instead of feeling like a bear inside, I felt like prey waiting to be pounced upon. I had started out in our new home with fearing the place we lived because of our van being

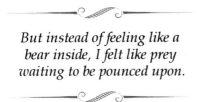

But instead of feeling like a bear inside, I felt like prey waiting to be pounced upon.

stolen, then progressed to fearing the state of my body, and now feared a potential stalker, which honestly made me start not to trust anyone new. I used to be the person who would listen to anyone's story, as long as it meant someone would be closer to Jesus. Because of the events that had occurred, the thought kept flooding my brain: "How can I trust anyone in my new town?" Land mine number three: fearing *all* people.

The wild and free little girl who had loved God and loved people started to believe that all people were out to get her. Since I had all these fears, there was nothing more to do but to keep all of us home as much as possible. We needed to keep our doors locked, avoid getting sick so that we wouldn't have to take medicine, and never go anywhere except the grocery store because we might run into a creeper; and if we did run into a creeper at the grocery store, I would just scream or kick them in the groin. I had it all planned out.

I started to share with my husband all the safety concerns that I had. I did not want our children corrupted, so I wanted to homeschool them. They would learn Scripture, not watch bad TV shows or movies, and be preachers before they were six, including being able to discern right and wrong spirits. They were going to be mighty warriors for Christ and not let anything get in their way — not even a little bit.

I had great intentions to teach them the right things, but now I can clearly see that my motives were not pure. I wanted control. I wanted my family safe. I wanted them close. I wanted everything that was most important to me within arm's reach. All this "control" that I thought I had left me irritable, unable to enjoy life, and unable to breathe, because life was too short and every day needed to be full. I thought that if I kept our days busy, I would not have to think about how torn I really was inside.

When we started homeschooling, it was extremely difficult because, like everything else I did, I had to do it with excellence. I wanted to adhere to a strict schedule, and when we would get off it, even just a little bit, I would get angry and start cleaning something, as if that was going to make things better. We would get even more behind, and then I would feel inadequate. I felt as if I wasn't a good mom or a good teacher. Once again I believed the awful lie that I couldn't do anything right. I was a mess — a hot mess. But I thought, "The kids are having fun, right?" *Wrong*!

I wish I could say that they were having a blast. Social media sure thought they were because I posted only the happy times of painting, scriptures learned, and all our smiles. Others did not get to see the frowning faces or the yelling because we had missed schedules again.These were some of the greatest moments of my life because my kids were learning about God, but they were also some of the worst times that haunt me still because they were learning about God from a mom who was not living out what she believed. She was scared, lost, and frozen.

In my last attempt to keep moving forward regardless of how I felt, I thought I would join another at-home business in order to feel of worth. I had to do something to help our family. Since I felt that I was failing at homeschooling and fell short daily as a wife, I really wanted to help us out financially.

Truth be told, I had done like four different at-home businesses in the past, and they all had failed, so I am not sure what I was thinking. But this one was something I was good at: working out. I could do that easily and encourage others to do the same. I could finally redeem my failed attempts and be of worth again. In addition, I could use the job as my ministry, to minister to others. I missed ministry.

Just like in all my other at-home businesses, I started out super enthusiastic. I got the websites, business cards, and shirts. If the business offered it, I bought it. I was going to make it work this time — along with having a rocking body. I immediately started to copy all that my up-line was doing in order to mirror them personally with their ideal bodies and their business in order to get where they were.

Seriously, they were making $100,000-plus a year, and I wanted to reach that goal so that my husband could have his dream. He wanted to go to seminary school so that one day he could become a pastor. I figured if I could be the breadwinner, it would take some pressure off him. He had always done all that he could to support me, and I wanted to return the favor. This meant countless hours on the computer, because most if not all of the business was online. I wanted this more than anything.

Somehow I was quickly back to where I had been in college, not the eating- disorder part, but with a crammed schedule. I would wake up at five in the morning to read my Bible, pray, work out, make videos of my workouts, have breakfast, clean up some, do school with the kids, play with the kids, have lunch made for them, do more school, let them nap while I did business stuff, make dinner, do laundry, do dishes, and then clean the schoolroom and get school stuff ready for the next day so that I could crash right afterwards to do it all over again. In the beginning, I was able to manage things pretty well, but something started to happen; the plates I was spinning on poles above me were starting to crash all around me. Land mine number four: fearing I would never measure up completely to anything—ever.

Before everything crashed completely, I decided to have a personal surgery. I know—absolutely insane! I could not believe myself either. Honestly, I really wanted to have it done, and not for any other reason but to finally do something to make myself feel good. In order to feel physically better and feel more like myself, I faced all my fears of medicine and doctors. But after I paid my money to have the surgery, I started to have this thought: "What if something happens to me during surgery and I die?"

I had struggled with thoughts of death before, but not to this magnitude. But we had kids now. If something happened to me, then they would grow up without a mom. I thought the surgery I was having was so selfish of me. How could I do this to my poor babies? I had myself so convinced that something was going to happen that I almost wrote a letter my kids "just in case." I never gained the strength to write the letter, but I did pray like crazy that nothing would happen to me.

To my surprise, nothing did. The surgery was a success, thankfully. I should have been able to leave all those fears behind me, right? *Wrong again!* After the surgery, I was told that I had an allergic reaction during the surgery. My fears grew greater than they had been at any other time in my life. I started to fear everything I did, as if death might happen at the next moment. I was lost. I desperately wanted to find myself. My husband wanted his wife back. My kids needed their mom back. I had no idea how to find that girl or woman again.

Land mine number five: I was scared to breathe, as if every breath would be my last. I was trapped and lay powerless. I was in another nightmare, screaming the loudest, but no one could hear me. I was unable to wake up and snap

out of it. I couldn't wake
myself up because I wasn't
asleep—I was in a living
nightmare. I did not care
about anyone else; I just
wanted to survive and get

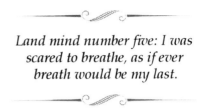

*Land mind number five: I was
scared to breathe, as if ever
breath would be my last.*

out of the trap in my mind that I was in alive.

Reflection:

*What are some of your biggest fears? Has fear every gripped your
life to the point of paralyzing your way of life? Are you aware that
fear is a HUGE faith killer and can keep you from reaching your
full potential in Christ? Are you also aware that God is big enough
to handle your fears?*

Scripture Focus:

*Joshua 1: 9, "Haven't I commanded you: be strong and coura-
geous? Do not be afraid or discouraged, for the LORD your God
is with you wherever you go."*

*Psalm 41: 10, "Do not fear, for I am with you; do not be afraid, for
I am your God. I will strengthen you; I will help you; I will hold
on to you with My righteous right hand."*

Psalm 94: 18-19, "If I say, "My foot is slipping," Your faithful love will support me, LORD. When I am filled with cares, Your comfort brings me joy.

CHAPTER 14: IN THE DESERT

It's like wishing for rain while standing in the desert.

~Author Unknown

Dehydrated . . . desperate for water without a drop in sight. The desert seemed to have no end, with mountains far above and valleys below. It appeared as an ocean of sand as far off as the horizon in the distance. Countless numbers of sand grains in every crevice of the skin caused it to crack and bleed and made the mouth feel like sandpaper, triggering it to thirst even more for water and the stomach to ache for much-needed food. Alone, with the unrelenting sun beating down upon His body and creating burns upon His skin, Jesus was at a very vulnerable point. He was extremely weak, and the enemy knew this all too well. The enemy chose to attack Jesus at this point, hoping to catch Him off guard. In spite of His weakened body and mind, Jesus was ready. He fought the devil through the Holy Spirit and the Word, and the enemy failed at his attempt.

Matthew 4:1 reveals, "Then Jesus was led by the Spirit into the wilderness to be tempted by the Devil." There was nothing that was going to stop the devil in his unmerciful pursuit to tempt Jesus, the Son of God. But no matter how great the devil's schemes were, on each account, Jesus denied him with boldness, lastly commanding, "Go away, Satan! For it is written: worship the Lord your God, and serve only Him" (Matthew 4: 10). I am amazed at the strength of the Savior. He stood up to the devil in one of His weakest moments. He had strength in the Holy Spirit through prayer, and He knew exactly how to respond to the enemy. He was ready. At the end of it all, after Jesus banished the enemy from His sight, angels came to tend to Jesus and His needs.

For a long time, I did not understand the reason the Lord was led into the desert to be tested by His archnemesis. No one would want to be Jesus in that moment — in the desert for forty days and forty nights, hungry, thirsty, and without a person in sight to lean on. However, Jesus knew something that I often forget: He knew that real freedom isn't free. He showed Satan over and over again that He would fight for His beloved church, even to the point of death, and in the end, He would crush Satan. His bride is everything to Him. He constantly reveals this by His unfailing love and grace, and through His unending prayers on her behalf, He fights.

Fight Club

Jesus has been constantly fighting for His bride, the body of Christ, since before time began. After his feet hit the earth, the dust that He used to help fashion man, He fought all the more. He rebuked Satan in the desert. Regardless of the number of people calling Him a liar, He told countless accounts of our Abba Father. He even sweat blood down His cheeks and suffered until He uttered the words "It is finished."Now He lives, having conquered death.

A dear friend of mine explains Jesus further: "One day we will see Him as He is, commanding a dreadful army of saints, mounted on a great white horse with His double-edged sword drawn and His white robe dripped in blood. Jesus is a warrior" (references to Revelation 19:11–16). We can always count on Jesus to fight.

I needed and still need to be reminded that even though Jesus constantly battles for me, I have to do my part and guard myself and fight with Him. The body of Christ is called to put on the full armor of God "so that you can stand against

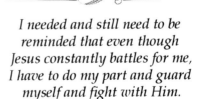

I needed and still need to be reminded that even though Jesus constantly battles for me, I have to do my part and guard myself and fight with Him.

the tactics of the Devil" (Ephesians 6:10), and "in every situation take the shield of faith, and with it you will be able to extinguish all the flaming arrows of the evil one" (Ephesians

6:14). I often let myself forget these truths. I let myself forget
that 1 Peter 5:8 warns me, "Be serious! Be alert! Your adver-
sary the Devil is prowling around like a roaring lion looking
for anyone he can devour."

Bone Dry

I was still stuck in a living nightmare without anything to
protect me. I was refusing help from God and His family, the
church, until I finally made a bold stand against the enemy.
On Easter Sunday in 2014, I was finally ready to face myself
in the mirror with a marker in my shaking hand. Our pastor
spoke an amazing message about Jesus and how He cleanses
us of our sin. I had never heard or seen the message of Jesus
painted so clearly in my entire life.

During the sermon, on the stage was a large mirror on a
chair. The pastor started to write on it with a red marker the
possible sins that we may have committed in our lifetimes. I
do not recall the exact words, but I am sure they were along
the lines of *lying, cheating, murder,* and a couple of others.
He took a rag and tried to wipe off the sins to demonstrate
how it is when we try to clean ourselves. However, when he
went to wipe away the words, they stayed; there were just
awful smeared marks all over the place, like a toddler trying
to clean up paint with a paintbrush.

Additionally, he took a hammer and smashed the glass,
startling everyone in the church, exclaiming, "This is what

Jesus does to our sin, our mess." He asked if there was any-thing we wanted to write on the extra mirrors in the front to give to Jesus, such as a sin that we had been carrying around with us. I started to walk down the aisle to write my word and to receive prayer as I had done many times before. But this time was different — it was a declaration.

I wrote the words *to live completely free*. I realized that day that even though I had been saved since I was thirteen years old, I had allowed a lot of things in my past to hold me down in ropes tied to the ground, like a chained dog. And by writing those words in front of me, I though, "Yay! I wrote the words down — that's it. I am totally free now!" I couldn't have been more wrong.

I wanted the true freedom that Christ provides. Ultimately, I knew Jesus had already won the final battle against the enemy through His death, but in that moment, I had no idea that in order to gain full freedom, I would have to fight through some things. They were intangible things, and they quickly became my battlefield.

Anxiety, panic attacks, OCD — oh my! I never knew what these things were, but to my surprise, all of them would be defined for me within three months of Easter. All the fears that I had stuffed in a closet for years were finally coming out, and it was dreadful. I felt like I was being constantly choked. I had gone through a lot of hard things in my life, but this was by far the hardest.

I had no idea that I was going to have to struggle for every bit of air that I breathed into my lungs. I feared medicine (even vitamins) and started to fear major- allergen foods. I feared that panic attacks were going to come at any moment and that the palpitations I was having were going to kick-start me into a heart attack and I could die at any time.

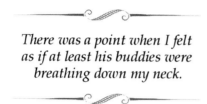

There was a point when I felt as if at least his buddies were breathing down my neck.

Now, I wasn't in the desert like Jesus, nor can I fathom having Satan literally standing beside me in person, in snake form, or however he appeared to Jesus. But I do know how it feels to be tormented by the flaming arrows of the enemy. There was a point when I felt as if at least his buddies were breathing down my neck.

I thought about death when I woke up in the morning, hung out with my family during the day, and when I forced my head to lie down to sleep. I mean, I knew that everyone dies at some point, but I was tired of thinking about it all the time. I felt like screaming until my voice grew hoarse from all my screams. I was so mad at all that I was facing because they were things that were intangible, and it was so hard to grab hold of them and heal from them.

Once again I hardly recognized myself. I felt like my eyes were sunken in from lack of sleep and peace. I just felt overall unhealthy — spiritually, mentally, and physically. I was thirsty for more of Jesus and hungry for the support of

His family. I needed His love, and I needed community with others in the body of Christ. Sadly, I was bone-dry.

I wanted the healing to be instant, as I mentioned earlier when discussing Ezekiel 37:4–6, when God commanded him to prophesy and the dry bones came to life: "He said to me, 'Prophesy concerning these bones and say to them: Dry bones, hear the word of the Lord! This is what the Lord God says to these bones: I will cause breath to enter you, and you will live. I will put tendons on you, make flesh grow on you, and cover you with skin. I will put breath in you so that you come to life. Then you will know that I am Yahweh.'"

I loved this truth because it reminded me how quickly God can work if He chooses to in order for individual battles to be won. I wanted this instant gratification in my situation. He had different plans for this girl, though. I had to start working as soon as that promise was put down on that mirror. The trouble was, like a boxer in a ring without a pair of gloves on or mouth guard or head protection, I started fighting unguarded, without the Word and the help of Jesus, the Holy Spirit, and others.

Reflection:

Have you ever had moments like this in your life when you were so desperate for God, His Word, and fellowship with other believers? Have you ever thought that maybe those moments in your life where your fault because you quit striving and fighting to pursue these things in your life? What kept you from striving for these things?

Scripture Focus:

2 Kings 3: 16-17, "Then he said, "This is what the Lord says: 'Dig ditch after ditch in this wadi.' For the Lord says, 'You will not see wind or rain, but the wadi will be filled with water, and you will drink — you and your cattle and your animals."

CHAPTER 15: RUNNING MASCARA

It hurts to let go, but sometimes it hurts more to hold on.
~Author Unknown

The pastor had just finished another message and asked everyone to bow their heads so that we could pray. I felt like it was the millionth time that I had heard the salvation prayer. My salvation had been secured for a long time, so my heart was at peace during that portion of the prayer. Then the pastor asked if there was anything in our lives holding us back from being everything that God created us to be. He challenged us further that if there was, we needed to raise our hands. I had been feeling fine throughout the entire message, until he asked that specific question. He may not have been asking that to anyone else in the room, but he was definitely talking to me.

A swarm of emotions came over me, and I started to tear up. I gained the strength to raise my hand. While the pastor prayed, I cried even more, trying to hide my sniffles and catch each tear before it dropped off my nose. But the tears were coming far too fast, and drops of black soon covered my hands. I literally felt the presence of the Lord all around me during that prayer, and I was thankful for the pastor leading it because it was exactly what I needed — I needed less of me and my issues and more of Jesus in my life.

After he said "amen," the band proceeded to play one last song, and I quickly tried to clean my face of any debris from my mascara. I turned to my husband and asked, "Do I have mascara all over my face?" He did a quick glance from top to bottom, left to right, and came back quickly with, "Nope, everything looks fine." Secretly I hoped and prayed that he was telling the truth instead of playing a joke. I didn't want to worry about all the faces I would have to pass by before helping with the youth group. I proceeded to walk out and had a few conversations, met with the youth leaders for prayer, and then made a mad dash to the bathroom to gain some *real* peace.

I ran into the lady's restroom, found the mirror, and thought, "Oh, thank the Lord. There really isn't anything on my face." If you know my husband, you know we like to play pranks back and forth, so I really didn't know what to expect when I found myself standing in front of the mirror with my reflection in front of me. But once I saw my reflection, another thought came to mind: "Why do I care? This is the one place that I am supposed to be able to be completely vulnerable, to be real with people and say out loud, 'I am a complete mess, and I need Jesus to fix me.'" Instead, I felt like I needed to hide everything that I was feeling on the inside that just happened to rear its ugly head that day.

A Glimpse In The Past

Furthermore, a handful of people already knew from a previous breakdown, or should I say "complete meltdown," eight weeks prior that something was not right in my life. I had been fighting serious anxiety, panic attacks, and new and irrational fears ever since I faced myself in the mirror Easter Sunday; so when the youth pastor spoke a few weeks after that about how friction in our lives is caused by an area we are not fully handing over to God and giving Him control of, my emotions were unhinged. I knew that I was a mess and part of the reason was because I was still trying to control everything in my life. In that moment, I felt tormented by the enemy, and I needed the church to literally come around me, lay hands on me, and pray. I broke down and lost all self-preservation. I knew that I could not stay in the place I was in, because I knew that a serious depression was to follow; however, moving forward to work on things was even scarier to me.

I cried so much that day that I felt like my head was going to explode. I could feel how the Lord had me set up for a "breakdown" moment that day; He had an appointment written in His book. I cried so long that by the time I was done, just one family plus my own was still left in the church. I was safe, surrounded by the family of God and God Himself. For being so broken, I finally got a glimpse of the peace that I had been longing for so deeply, through a sweet sister's prayer.

Back to the Future

I stood in the girls restroom in front of the mirror on this new Sunday morning, wondering how I could feel so safe as to express my fears and shortcomings one week, but so quick to hide them the next. In that instant, I was tired of pretending like I had it all together. I was tired of trying to be perfect. All that my fight for perfection had done to me throughout my entire life was to drive me to the ground. My lifelong battle to fit into a cookie-cutter image had left me barren and in desperate need of my Savior and His body.

> *I felt like I had to stay strong and hold it together, let others know that I was okay and didn't need any help, as if I were a super-Christian who never fell at all, so that I could lift others up.*

In all seriousness, I felt like an older sister trying to keep it together for her younger siblings. I felt like I had to stay strong and hold it together, let others know that I was okay and didn't need any help, as if I were a super-Christian who never fell at all, so that I could lift others up. I thought that struggling meant that I didn't have enough faith and that I didn't think God was big enough, strong enough, or cared enough about me to help.

There were other questions that haunted me and nagged at me, playing like loud drums in my mind as they had in my past. Would Jesus love me if I admitted that I wasn't perfect? Would the church accept me in the same way if I finally said I needed help? I thought that since I was broken, God couldn't use me in ministry anymore. Was I going to have to sit on the sidelines from now on and watch others walk in their strength and calling? I was so tired of being tormented by all these lies from the enemy. I needed to see the true light once again shining forth for me in my extremely dark situation.

As I left the mirror, I longed for church to be over as quickly as possible so that I could hide from others and sort out all of the junk in my mind. In the course of that day, as I struggled with my landslide of thoughts, the Lord reminded me of the words of Paul in 2 Corinthians 12:1–10. His words gave me a taste of freedom by reminding me of my human nature: that I will never be flawless on this side of eternity and that there will always be something to deal with to constantly point me to God's strength instead of my own.

2 Corinthians 12: 1-10 reads:

> Boasting is necessary. It is not profitable, but I will move on to visions and revelations of the Lord. I know a man in Christ who was caught up into the third heaven 14 years ago. Whether he was in the

body or out of the body, I don't know, God knows. I know that this man—whether in the body or out of the body I don't know, God knows—was caught up into paradise. He heard inexpressible words, which a man is not allowed to speak. I will boast about this person, but not about myself, except of my weaknesses. For if I want to boast, I will not be a fool, because I will be telling the truth. But I will spare you, so that no one can credit me with something beyond what he sees in me or hears from me, especially because of the extraordinary revelations. Therefore, so that I would not exalt myself, a thorn in the flesh was given to me, a messenger of Satan to torment me so I would not exalt myself. Concerning this, I pleaded with the Lord three times to take it away from me. But He said to me, "My grace is sufficient for you, for power is perfected in weakness." Therefore, I will most gladly boast all the more about my weaknesses, so that Christ's power may reside in me. So I take pleasure in weaknesses, insults, catastrophes, persecutions, and in pressures, because of Christ. For when I am weak, then I am strong.

I remember reading this passage of Scripture many times before, when I was growing up, but it wasn't until I started to go through intangible things such as anxiety that I realized that all the hard things may not ever go away until I get to heaven. Do I desire to be set free from everything? Yes! Is it a bad thing to want to be healed? Absolutely not! But what if the healing doesn't come? Do I turn away from God? Do

I continue with a mind-set of God doesn't love me or can't use me because I am broken? Through Paul's words, I know that is a resounding *no*. His words challenged me to have a different outlook, but the awakening didn't come with ease.

Reflection:

Have you ever been afraid to let others know that you weren't that strong and needed help? Where you afraid of how you would look as a person by admitting you weren't perfect and couldn't do everything on your own?

Scripture Focus:

2 Corinthians 12: 9, "But He said to me, "My grace is sufficient for you, for power is perfected in weakness." Therefore, I will most gladly boast all the more about my weaknesses, so that Christ's power may reside in me."

Part 5

WHITE FLAGS

Then you will know the truth, and the truth will set you free.

~John 8:32

We raise our white flags
The war is over
Love has come
Your love has won.

~Chris Tomlin
White Flag

CHAPTER 16: SURRENDER

Surrender to what is, let go of what was,
have faith in what will be.

~Sonia Ricotti
Author, Motivational Speaker

My heart pounded uncontrollably within my chest. I couldn't breathe. My throat was tight, I felt dizzy, and I just knew that I was going to pass out. Thoughts of panic flashed through my mind: "Am I having a heart attack? Am I going to die?" I was scared. I was alone, and no one else was around to call on for help. I did all that I knew to do in order to stay calm, but I couldn't calm down. All I could do was stumble to the phone and dial 911.

The ambulance came to my rescue right as my husband got home. They said that I was probably fine, but I was too afraid to just stay home and accept their words as truth. What if my heart started up again? What if I was really having a heart attack? I needed assurance as soon as possible, so they took me to the hospital. I waited as best I knew how, surrounded by unfamiliar faces in the waiting room behind the emergency-room doors. I wasn't crazy! I knew something was wrong with me. I just had to know the answers.

As I sat in the waiting room, feeling helpless and all alone because my husband had to stay in the main lobby, the Lord used a man to speak to me. He was in a wheelchair and could barely speak. When he did speak, he had to use one of those voice boxes, which made him sound like a robot. Before he was able to utter any words to me, he coughed, shook, and fell to the floor. I cried out to a nurse in fear for this man's life and of course because I was freaking out inside about my own well being too. Once the nurses situated this man back into his chair, he glanced over at me and spoke as confidently as his box would let him: "Everything is going to be okay, honey. There is nothing to fear; everything is going to be all right." A sense of peace came over me.

After a few hours passed, they finally got to me, and I was able to see the nurse. She checked my heart rate and asked me the series of events that had taken place just some time before. I tried to convince her that something was wrong, but she said, "Honey, it sounds like you had an anxiety attack." I was furious. I was so tired of hearing about anxiety! I wanted to punch a wall. I thought, "Could people please stop talking about anxiety, before I lose it!" I wanted to act like a "terrible

202

two" toddler who was trying not to listen to her parents, cover my ears, and sing the "la, la, la" song. I was so done.

The doctor came in with an EKG machine to check everything that was going on beneath the surface. It took about five minutes to hook up the machine, but only about five seconds to do the test. He studied the findings and gently said, "Honey, I think you had a panic attack." Thoughts taunted me automatically: "Seriously, what is a panic attack anyway? Is it just my body's way of shouting to everyone that this girl is crazy?"

I had no idea what to think of all the events that had occurred. Instead of being happy that nothing was physically wrong with me, I was mad—mad that there wasn't anything to point to in order to blame my issues. My husband took me to the car, and believe it or not, I cried like I had never cried before. Luckily, this time there wasn't any makeup to try to wipe from my face. My husband asked, trying not to step on a land mine himself, "Tiffany, honey, what is going on with you?" I didn't know how to respond because I didn't know how to put into words all that I was feeling inside.

Finally, everything came out abruptly. I told him through my waterfall of tears, "I just feel like a crazy person. Am I crazy? Anxiety, I don't have anxiety. I am tired of people talking about anxiety. I am just done. Something else is wrong. The surgery I chose to do did this to me. Something has to be to blame. The doctors need to figure out what is going on instead of labeling me like this. I am tired of being labeled. What if something is wrong and they are missing it because they are labeling me? *I am losing it!"*

My loving husband grabbed my hand and said with all the hesitation in the world, wondering if I was going to snap back at him or not, "Tiffany, you have always had anxiety, honey. The way that all of this is manifesting may be different for you now, but you have always had this. You even had a panic attack before, when we first got married. You may not remember, but you did. Honey, this has just gotten really bad lately. We need to do something about all of this. I am concerned."

I wanted to bury my head in a pillow and scream. Thoughts came like a tornado, causing all kinds of distress and debris: "How will I be able to do anything about this issue? I have two kids with me all the time. We don't have any family around, so who do I run to if I get scared? What if I have one of these panic attacks when the kids are around, and I pass out and die from lack of air, and they are left afraid? Why does this bother me so much? Why is it such a big deal to be labeled with anxiety? All it means is that I have to work through something else. The Lord has me, so I don't understand why I am shaken to the core."

The Beautiful Letdown

Yes, it was apparent I had a problem. Anxiety was my new nemesis. Daily it haunted me, keeping me from having complete joy in life. I started to do what the enemy plans for those who are trapped by fear: I began to isolate myself even more from everyone who loved me and from those I loved. I didn't want others to see me struggle or think that I was weak. I didn't want people to think I was crazy either. I didn't know what people would think of me if they knew that anxiety was my struggle. Would they still accept me, or would they turn away because they wouldn't want to talk to me anymore?

I also questioned God's goodness. I often wondered why I had to be the one to go through this. I thought He was punishing me because of some irrational decisions I had made or because I constantly fell short of everything He asked me to do. I started to think that I could handle it all alone. I didn't want help. Furthermore, I didn't have a problem. Admitting that I had a problem meant admitting that something about me was defective. But I was bursting at the seams…I couldn't lie to myself, or those around me any longer.

I finally realized I was shattered glass. Throughout my entire life, I had worked hard to pick up the pieces to this glass that had been dropped, but all I kept doing by trying to pick up

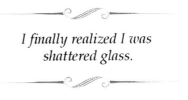

I finally realized I was shattered glass.

the pieces alone was to cut my fingers over and over again and reopen scars developed over time. Since I couldn't glue my life back together, even after I accepted the Lord into my life, I pretended to be a perfect Christian, which led me to want to be the best in body, mind, and spirit. All these things left me exhausted and tired of covering up my pain, pretending like I had everything all together.

But I didn't have it all together. I finally decided to raise the white flag of surrender. I had my white flag up, waving it back and forth with all my might...laying down all of my rights—to be in control, to stay strong, to keep playing the game of perfectionism. I was done trying to be the strong one. I wanted to be the weak one and let Jesus and His strength shine through me in order to help others.

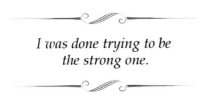

I was done trying to be the strong one.

I realized all that I had been doing for my entire life was trying to fix myself instead of letting Jesus fix me. By trying to do this, I wasn't leaving any room for Jesus. I had thought, "I can do everything without Him. I can be the perfect picture of a Christian and show others how it is done. I don't need any help." I was wrong. Romans 8:8 reminded me of this truth, revealing, "So, then, those who are in the flesh cannot please God." Even though I had Jesus in my life, I remained in the flesh and lived according to the flesh by keeping my mind focused on the things of the flesh (see Romans 8:5). Nothing I did pleased Him because I was trying to do everything without Him. I realized that nothing was perfect apart from Him. I needed to remain in Him. I needed Him, and I still do today. We all do.

Reflection:

*Have you completely surrendered everything in your life to Jesus –
all of your best and all of your worst? Do you realize that you
are nothing with out Him and that by acting like you have it all
together is only hurting yourself?*

Scripture Focus:

*Job 1:20-21, "Then Job stood up, tore his robe, and shaved his head.
He fell to the ground and worshiped, saying: Naked I came from
my mother's womb, and naked I will leave this life. The Lord gives,
and the Lord takes away. Praise the name of Yahweh.*

CHAPTER 17: STARVING THE BODY

A hungry stomach cannot hear.

~Jean de La Fontaine

When I had anorexia, it was easy to walk in denial. I just knew I was fine; I didn't have a problem. I just had this picture in my mind of what I wanted to fashion myself into, and I was going to obtain the air-brushed look like the women on the covers of magazines if it was the last thing I did. I was going to obtain it regardless of the cost, whether that meant missing meals, not cutting corners on my exercising, regurgitating to get rid of excess calories when I did overeat, or buying the right clothes. I was going to look the part, even though I knew that the perfect body didn't exist.

I realized that I had overworked at my attempt when my nephew hugged me for the first time in a long time. He wrapped his tiny arms around me and voiced, "Aunt Tiffany, I can put my arms all the way around you. You are so skinny that I can feel your ribs." Like a lightning bolt to the body, those words stung all over, and I was awakened to the fact that I had failed horribly. One day I was beefed up with muscles, and the next day I was caught by my nephew for being too skinny. He was just six years old at the time. I knew the Lord was speaking through him, and I knew I couldn't continue the trend I was on, because not only was I starving myself, but I was being a poor example to those closest to me. I asked myself, "What are you doing?" I knew then that I needed to quit starving my body.

> *I asked myself, "What are you doing?" I knew then that I needed to quit starving my body.*

The Cold Hard Truth

There is a question I have for the church, the body of Christ. Are we starving the body of what it really needs? Truly, I believe with all confidence that we are. I believe we are failing not only those outside the church walls, but also those inside the church walls. We wear our masks, making out like we are perfect and have everything together, but in hindsight, we are all broken messes and need Jesus constantly. Like I did, the church is doing all that it can to maintain an airbrushed image of a perfect church, which doesn't exist on this side of eternity.

Even though we know the truth, we as a church do all that we can in order to obtain the unattainable — whether that means missing prayer time in order to fine-tune worship songs so that the rows will be filled and crowds will be happily tapping their feet because this is their "jam," cutting Scripture short to make it fit our personal message in order to make us feel comfortable, or weeding out the "troublemakers" within the walls whenever the "real saints" get a little uneasy. We even try to buy all the right things, such as decorations, lights, sound — and who can forget the coffee? If there is no coffee, then the entire congregation might be a little irritable, and that just can't be, because new people might leave if they are. Seriously, it's absurd! There is so much that we are missing here. I wonder how Jesus really feels about the church of today. Is He angry? Is He weeping for her because she is doing everything except what He called her to do? Where has His beloved bride gone wrong?

Out of Focus

Ezekiel 34 was originally written to the shepherds of Israel. God was fed up with them because they were not doing their job of taking care of His people. He was at a raging point, an angry God. He declared these things in verses 1–4:

> The word of the Lord came to me: "Son of man, prophesy against the shepherds of Israel. Prophesy, and say to them: This is what the Lord God says

to the shepherds: Woe to the shepherds of Israel, who have been feeding themselves! Shouldn't the shepherds feed their flock? You eat the fat, wear the wool, and butcher the fattened animals, but you do not tend the flock. You have not strengthened the weak, healed the sick, bandaged the injured, brought back the strays, or sought the lost. Instead, you have ruled them with violence and cruelty."

After reading this passage, it is easy to say, "Man, God was really angry at those shepherds. I am glad that I wasn't one of them." But church, aren't we the shepherds of today? Are we not called to be Jesus to the world around us? Instead, all we can do is try to calculate when Jesus will come back, whose church is bigger, and argue over which Bible is the correct version to use. None of these things matter to God. His purpose matters, and that purpose still remains...to bring as many people as we can to Jesus.

Luke 19:10 reads "For the Son of Man has come to seek and to save the lost." Matthew 28:18–20 reveals: "Go therefore and make disciples of all nations, baptizing them in the name of the Father and of the Son and of the Holy Spirit, teaching them to observe all that I have commanded you. And behold, I am with you always, to the end of the age." How

Instead of bringing people to Jesus, we just scatter them and run them off away from Jesus by focusing on all the wrong things.

can we seek the lost and make disciples if we are doing just the opposite? Instead of bringing people to Jesus, we just scatter them and run them off away from Jesus by focusing on all the wrong things.

Ezekiel 34:5-6 explains this further by describing how people were being scattered for lack of a shepherd and became food for all the wild animals. The flock was scattered, and there "was no one searching or seeking for them" (verse 6). We are allowing God's beloved children or possible beloved children to be devoured by the world because we the church, the body of Christ, are not seeking the ones who are weak, sick, need bandaging, have gone astray, or are lost.

As Jesus' bride, we are doing such a poor job because we are too busy asking questions such as "How can I be fed more? When can someone do something for me? What can make me stronger? Why don't they ever say Hi to me?" Or even worse we think to ourselves, "I am much better than her because she didn't read her bible at all this week. He is so lazy because he didn't do any of his bible study. Their children are out of control because they were arguing as they came into the church building. Look at her clothes... she looks like a homeless person, I thought her husband had a good job."

We are blinded to what people really need inside and outside the church because we are too focused on ourselves. Individually, we are too busy taking the perfect "selfie" to post with a scripture on social media to make ourselves look holy, or collectively we make it our personal mission to make sure that the church we are a part of doesn't miss a spin on the hamster wheel of refinement. Church, we are truly missing the point.

The Beggar

Here is an illustration to help paint a picture of all that we are doing as the body of Christ, followers of Jesus. When I was in eighth grade, I had the privilege to see an amazing drama at Acquire the Fire, a youth gathering created by Ron Luce. I can still close my eyes and see it played out in front of me, because it impacted me greatly. Picture three people spread out on the stage. The person in the middle speaks and has a stale piece of bread. When she speaks, she is sarcastic and begins to complain about her bread and the fact that it is extremely nasty and of course hard. She could not care less about eating her bread. She wishes she could have a burger or something else. She is ungrateful.

On the far right of the stage, there is a girl who does not have any bread in her midst. She is begging for something to eat. She is even begging for the stale piece of bread next to her. She is desperate — desperate for just a taste. She screams and begs for someone to come by and hand her something because she is starving and doesn't have any source of food around her. No one comes to her rescue. She is all alone and afraid for her well-being. She has no hope.

The boy on the far left of the stage is standing there with a whole loaf of bread. He is enjoying every single piece of bread, but instead of sharing it with the girl who has none or giving the "stale bread" girl a fresh new taste, he begs for more. Before the crowd can get out one more laugh because of how obnoxiously comical he is being about it, something happens from above: a very large quantity of bread is dropped from the top and dumps all over the young man. Again, instead of sharing his sea of food, he begins to laugh, smile, and literally swim in his truck-load of bread. He loves the new bread even though he

> *He loves the new bread even though he was perfectly full and content with all that he already had. He is fat with the gospel, the only real source of hope.*

was perfectly full and content with all that he already had. He is fat with the gospel, the only real source of hope.

A Slap To The Face

When watching this drama for the first time, it was easy to laugh along, but as the years have gone by the truth has set in, a swarm of conviction has swam over every ounce of my brain. Church, what are we doing? We sit in our church, the "perfect body", and starve it of what it really needs because we are too focused on other things. We also continue to be poor examples to those who could be a part of the body. But, who would want to be part of the body with the way that we act? We starve everyone of what they need the most, the one we all need the most, and that is more of Jesus.

Jesus wasn't interested in perfection, like the church of today is. In earlier chapters, we saw clearly that instead of turning His face away from "messy" people, He not only welcomed the mess, but He also went towards it as described in Matthew 9:36: "When He saw the crowds, He felt compassion for them, because they were weary and worn out, like sheep without a shepherd."

Jesus went to be with people no matter what kind of mess was going to meet Him or what kind of "wrong" people were in the crowd.

Jesus went to be with people no matter what kind of mess was going to meet Him or what kind of "wrong" people were in the crowd. Jud White, senior pastor at Central Christian Church, once said, "Jesus hung out with the 'wrong' people to show them that it didn't matter if they were the 'right' or 'wrong' people. Regardless, they could be His people." Jesus made us His people when we didn't deserve it at all. We need to do better at accepting the muck inside ourselves and around us so that more people can see the true heart of our Savior. He desires to have everyone in His family.

We need to ask ourselves the question…does the church need to refocus and change the way it operates today? Some people may argue that I am wrong and that the church of today is totally fine and doesn't need to change its ways, because it's healthy. Although, I feel as if the body of Christ is in denial and if the body of Christ were honest with itself, the truth would come forth that it's not. If the mind-set continues that it is healthy, the church will stop striving towards Jesus, and people will continue to be driven away from Jesus instead of to Him. Driving people away from Jesus is the last thing we want to do.

Reflection:

Would Jesus be happy with us as individual followers of Christ and collectively as the church today? Are we driving people away from the church because they will never rise to the occasion based on the perfect masks we wear and the measuring sticks we have created? Are we just trying to build up the numbers of our church by putting on a show in order to feed our own egos instead of offering more of Jesus?

Scripture Focus:

2 Peter 3: 9, "The Lord does not delay His promise, as some understand delay, but is patient with you, not wanting any to perish but all to come to repentance."

Romans 3: 9, "What then? Are we any better? Not at all! For we have previously charged that both Jews and Gentiles are all under sin, as it is written: There is no one righteous, not even one."

CHAPTER 18: WHAT CHURCH?

We need to stop giving people excuses not to believe in God.
You've probably heard the expression 'I believe in God,
just not organized religion'.
I don't think people would say that if the church truly
lived like we are called to live.

~Francis Chan

Crazy Love

I have regrets over the course of my life, but one of my biggest regrets in life is how I treated a couple of my best friends, Julie and Caroline. We were in the tenth grade; I had just gotten my new "egg on wheels" for my sixteenth birthday, and we did everything together. We were joined at the hip, and most people thought we were sisters. We all had blonde hair that fell to our shoulders and spent as much time together as possible. We rode four-wheelers, flirted with boys, played basketball, chased each other around Julie's pond, cruised in her Jeep to the beach, and terrorized Caroline's younger brother as often as possible. I loved my friends as much as I did my family. I just knew that our friendship would last forever.

Since we were so close, I didn't want Julie and Caroline to just be my friends in this life; I wanted them to meet Jesus and have a friend for eternity. After some time, I worked up the courage to invite them to church. We did everything else together, so I thought, "Why not worship together?" They had said many times that church wasn't for them at all, but this time was different. This time they said *yes*! I was so thrilled to have them agree to go with me. I just knew they were going to love it as much as I did. I wanted and longed for my friends to know about Jesus and to have a relationship with Him like I had.

I waited impatiently until the Sunday that they were going to go with me had finally arrived. The morning was filled with sunshine and pancakes that my stepdad made for breakfast. Life was good, and it was about to get better because church was right in front of us. We headed in, the three amigos, and said hello to our usual hangout people from school, who also went to my church. Julie and Caroline found a place on the lounge couches in the youth room, and my youth pastor called me to the side. I thought he was going to say how exited he was to see my friends, but I was wrong.

A Rock In A Hard Place

He said, "Hey, Tiffany. I am so glad that you brought some friends with you this morning to join us. It's always great to see new faces here. But there is one thing I was hoping you could do. I was wondering if you could tell them that their shorts are way too short to wear here. You need to let them know that the next time they come, they should definitely wear something else."

A great battle began inside me. I had no idea how he expected me to tell my best friends this news about their Daisy Dukes. They were my friends, though, so I thought, "Of course they will understand and not be mad at me." But then I wondered if maybe I could just pretend to tell them, and it wouldn't be that big of a deal. I could lie. Thinking thoroughly, I knew I couldn't do that at all. I couldn't sweep it under the table. I couldn't lie to my youth pastor and say I would tell them but then not tell them. I was a youth assistant to the youth leader, so I couldn't let him down. Plus, I kind of agreed that their shorts were a little short for church. I just knew that my friends would understand.

I took a deep breath, making sure that oxygen filled every part of my body, before I walked slowly to my beautiful friends. As soon as I got to them and opened my mouth, I quickly regretted my decision. Julie's and Caroline's faces were filled with embarrassment, anger, and disgust. I couldn't believe that the words actually came out of my mouth: "Julie and Caroline, the next time you girls come to church with me, you need to wear something different. Your shorts are way too short for this place."

I wish I could say that they were not offended by what I said and that they came back to church with me but, the facial expressions they had were the tell-all, and they never came to church with me again. Furthermore, my forever friends slowly became a distant memory. After that incident, they hardly spoke to me anymore. We parted ways in what felt like the instant my harsh words were spoken.

I missed my friends, my best friends. Even more important, I knew I had messed up. I had missed the perfect opportunity to share the true Jesus with my sweet sisters. Even more so, I do not know if they have ever stepped foot into a church again. Through my one action, they got a bad taste in their mouths about it all, and I will never know if or when that will ever wash away.

Because of my quick tongue and judgmental heart, two very important people in my life turned away from the church, but even more important, they turned away from Jesus, the one person they would most need in life.

Because of my quick tongue and judgmental heart, two very important people in my life turned away from the church, but even more important, they turned away from Jesus, the one person they would most need in life. I hate that I was an instrument used in their lives for them to despise the church, the body of Christ, and Jesus. Needless to say, I have experienced the whiplash of hurting amazing people in my life. I turned them away from the most peaceful, loving person in the universe — Jesus Himself. I know firsthand how the church can be used as a tool of distress.

Say What?

What is church? To my friends, or to my tenth-grade self's "ex-friends," the church represented a place that they despised. It was a place of judgment where they couldn't even dress the way they wanted and remain comfortable. The place where they should have been fully accepted and loved regardless of their dress quickly became the place that they were cast aside and called out in front of others, leaving them embarrassed and ashamed.

Alas, there are countless numbers of stories such as this one, which is a PG version, by the way. I know there are many stories even worse than this one that represent the church and how people are treated by the body of Christ. Through these experiences, over and over again people are becoming fed up with Christians altogether, both individually and collectively. In return, the bride of Christ is hurting the heart of the Savior. Instead of becoming vehicles of love, the body of Christ has become a body of bullies.

The believers stand in the parking lot waiting for the church doors to swing wide open in order to receive a fresh word to get fat on. Once the church doors open, a mob charges in through the doors, shoving and throwing elbows to catch the best seat to be fed another great message to place in their back pockets and to never be used again; worship with angelic, beautiful voices; and hope that someone doesn't know about the fight that just happened with their family on the way to church or the other struggles they fight in secret. All the while the so called, imperfect, slow to faith, nonconformists, and outsiders are left trampled in the dust with their aches and pains and have no one

All the while the so called, imperfect, slow to faith, nonconformists, and outsiders are left trampled in the dust with their aches and pains and have no one but the sidewalk to share in their hopelessness.

but the sidewalk to share in their hopelessness. I can say all this without a shadow of doubt because I have been both the judge and the judged. I know that the church, without even realizing it, leaves the Calebs, Rickys, Susans, Julies, Carolines, and many others on the outside to remain bone-dry with out a Heavenly Father and His family.

In all seriousness, what has happened to the church, the bride of Christ that Christ died on the cross for, the body of believers that used to be a group of individuals that loved Jesus and loved others? Over the course of time, the love has slowly faded…for Christ, His bride, and others on the outside. During the time that Jesus walked the earth, the body didn't care about who had issues. All they cared about was pointing people to the One who would love them and accept them in spite of their shortcomings, flaws, and to lead them to a better life while simultaneously healing them from their issues. Sadly, the church has slowly started to blend in with the rest of the world. The church is great at faking their concern for others all the while focusing on self and building themselves up, making it seem as if they are better than everyone else. Don't believe me? Catch a glimpse of how services have changed throughout the centuries.

All About Jesus

When Jesus gave sermons during His time on the filth of the earth, there were no praise-and-worship bands, drama segues, comfortable chairs, or pulpits. There were mountains in the backdrop, and Jesus spoke with love and authority. There were rocks to sit on for cushioning as the heat of the day beat down on everyone's back. The people hungered for fresh words from the Lord. People wanted more and more in spite of what it would reveal about them personally.

They knew they were imperfect and in desperate need of a Savior to change them. They wanted a front-row seat to the only man who had ever walked or ever will walk in perfection. They had been waiting on Jesus for quite some time, and they were not interested in letting Him go. They followed Him everywhere. They did not try to wear a mask to pretend that they had it all together. Even if they had tried, they knew that Jesus would see their brokenness for all that it was and love them anyway. The multitude of people, or the megachurch of Jesus' time, wanted and needed more of Him.

Church back then was just that: following, loving, and begging for more of the Savior. People would walk miles and search for Him to catch just one glimpse of His face or to grab just a piece of His garment. People knew that if they could just get to Jesus, He would make everything better. Where has the church gone wrong? In the generations following Jesus' time on earth, has the church lost its main focus of His life, death, and resurrection?

The Paradigm Is Shifting

The focus has been put on so many unimportant things, such as numbers. Exactly how big can a church get? Now, don't get me wrong. Big churches, or megachurches, are used in amazing ways for the Lord, and they have their place. The problem is when every other church tries to mimic their every move. The smaller church may think, "If we can just have the light show that the megachurches have, if we can have a better sound system, if we can have the perfect worship leader or the best speaker, then maybe we will have the attendance that those churches have, more people will get saved, and the church will grow."

When churches operated in this manner, people outside the church might start to have the wrong idea about Jesus and think that if they act better, look better, do better, and have all the bells and whistles, then Jesus will love them. The church collectively is giving false hope to people, making them chase after perfectionism instead of running to Jesus, the author and perfecter of faith (Hebrews 12:2). As a result, people are lost, tired, worn, and frustrated.

Furthermore, the church service has become a show for people to col- lectively watch and offer their praise or criticism con-

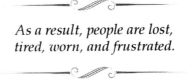

As a result, people are lost, tired, worn, and frustrated.

cerning what the church did or didn't do. Instead of focusing on Jesus and His message, embracing broken brothers and sisters in Christ in all walks of life, the church easily picks each other apart just like society does. Words come up in con- versation of who could have sung that song better or danced more on cue, whether or not the pastor taught everything spot-on without fault, wondering "What in the world was she wearing?" and the list goes on. No, wonder people don't want to step inside the church walls.

Members of the church, Christians, have become specta- tors, and that is why the bride of Christ has slowly become the most hated people on the planet. Unbelievers are doing their best to find comfort or salvation in other religions or in worldly things that will never satisfy them in this life or the next. The church needs to wake up because it is being a poor representation of Jesus.

Instead of admitting failures, shortcomings, and relying on Jesus for everything, the church has become like gods.

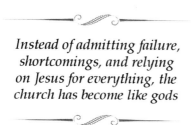

Instead of admitting failure, shortcomings, and relying on Jesus for everything, the church has become like gods

The people of the church decides who can come to church and who cannot by who is invited. When a person doesn't look like they belong in the church, the Family of God, they are left out. When a person has a habit that would reflect poorly on the church collectively, no one takes the step to invite "those people," in order keep up the ideal façade.

I know that Jesus is not happy with the church today. Now I am not saying that there are not *any* good churches or Christians out there today, because I know that there are. But with every horrible experience that exists within a church or the people within a church, it is easy to see that the body of Christ fails constantly. For this reason alone, the body of Christ constantly needs Jesus, not all of the things it chooses to focus on. The church is filled with imperfect people and always will be no matter how great the stride, as we have learned, until heaven reveals itself. So why is it a constant temptation for the church to represent itself as flawless before the world? All that does is push the rest of the world out because of *their* blemishes, and that is not God's design for the church at all.

Reflection:

Have you ever been asked to leave a church because you did not act, look, or talk like everyone else in the church? Have you ever asked someone to leave the church because they did not act, look, or talk like everyone else? How do you think that God feels about both of these situations?

Scripture Focus:

John 8: 1-11, "At dawn He went to the temple complex again, and all the people were coming to Him. He sat down and began to teach them. Then the scribes and the Pharisees brought a woman caught in adultery, making her stand in the center. "Teacher," they said to Him, "this woman was caught in the act of committing adultery. In the law Moses commanded us to stone such women. So what do You say?" They asked this to trap Him, in order that they might have evidence to accuse Him. Jesus stooped down and started writing on the ground with His finger. When they persisted in questioning Him, He stood up and said to them, "The one without sin among you should be the first to throw a stone at her." Then He stooped down again and continued writing on the ground. When they heard this, they left one by one, starting with the older men. Only He was left, with the woman in the center. When Jesus stood up, He said to her, "Woman, where are they? Has no one condemned you?" "No one, Lord," she answered. "Neither do I condemn you," said Jesus. "Go, and from now on do not sin anymore."

CHAPTER 19: FREEDOM

We build too many walls and not enough bridges.

~Sir Isaac Newton

One of the hardest things I have ever had to do was to admit that on this side of eternity, I would always be incomplete in some way or another. After years of striving for excellence and failing, I was able to completely give in to the perfect love of the heavenly Father and accept His constantly helping hand. The seas parted and dry land appeared, just as the seas parted in Exodus so that Moses could lead and free a generation of people from their former bondage. I was finally able to look beyond myself. For the first time in a long time, I was moved with compassion. The moment happened at a time that I least expected it. I was actually doing my best to avoid people in order to focus on my own problems, but Jesus had different plans for me. Like a train running on the train tracks and bursting through a brick wall, the moment hit me without any warning at all…

As the train came at me, the moments around me were moving in slow motion as if I were stuck in the worst kung-fu movie ever, where actions move swiftly but speech lags behind. I did my normal routine at church that particular morning. The kids and I went to our mandatory "donuts galore" meeting, and then we headed for a potty break before service. They went off to class, and I headed off to sit in our usual seat, trying to do my best to talk to the smallest number of people as possible because it had been a pretty hectic week in my "anxiety girl" world. As I went to sit down, I glanced to the back row in the dimly lit sanctuary, and it was like a spotlight was directly on . . . her.

The woman seemed to want to be left alone, like me, but instead of walking around with a smile and pretending like all was dandy as I did, she sat with all-black clothing on, like she was at the wrong place and there should have been a casket in our midst. She made her head sink lower and tried not to make eye contact with anyone. She wanted to be left alone, but at the same time, it was as if she were screaming for someone to pay attention to her. She needed a breakthrough, but no one cared to turn a head. She seemed full of shame and despair. The Lord told me to go talk to her, and I thought, "Lord, I am a mess. How in the world can I help this woman?" I started to walk back to her while having this back-and-forth with the Holy Spirit. I had no idea what I was going to say to her.

I reached her with my heart skipping around, and I asked her if I could sit beside her. Once I was granted permission,

I asked if she had been attending the church for a while or if it was her first time. I was so ashamed of her answer. She explained that she had been going to the church for a while, and that this particular Sunday was actually going to be her last. I didn't have the heart to tell her that I had never seen her in my life. How had I missed this woman, especially with the way she looked so downcast? I felt so responsible for walking past her week after week.

Our conversation continued. "So, is everything okay?" I asked, not expecting her elongated answer.

"No, everything is awful. My husband and I are getting a divorce, and it has resulted in me having to leave town and be away from my kids. He was unfaithful for the last time in our marriage. I just couldn't take it anymore." With tears pouring down her face, she continued: "I hate this. I don't want to leave my children. I really do not want to leave him, but he wants nothing to do with me. I really want to work it out with him, but he doesn't want to. He used to be a devoted Christian, and now he could not care less about God. I am torn."

I tried my best to keep my mouth closed during her gut-wrenching story. I felt so bad for her. More importantly, I felt terrible that she had been sitting in the church, probably going through all that alone, and now she was leaving town. I wished I had seen her sooner and provided comfort for her sooner, but I did the best I could do in that moment. I asked her if I could pray for her, and she agreed. After I prayed, I slowly went back to my seat, having the hardest time leaving her. I could tell that she needed a moment to herself. The entire time I sat in service, all I could think about was the woman—Nicole.

I sat on the edge of my seat for the entire service in hopes of catching up with her before she left church so that I could get some contact information from her. I wanted so badly to stay in touch with her and to be there for her. But as soon as the service ended, I jerked my head around, and in the blink of an eye, she was gone. I was so upset with myself. I could have handled that situation better. I could have sat with her, asked for her number before I left her, or asked her to come sit with me. My forehead met my palm many times that day. I shouldn't have left her side. I thought, "Did she really need time to herself?"

> Then the Lord quickly whispered in my spirit: "The church and this world are full of Nicoles, Tiffany. She is just one of many."

Then the Lord quickly whispered in my spirit: "The church and this world are full of Nicoles, Tiffany. She is just one of many." In that moment, I thanked God for Nicole. She was used to remind me once again that I was not the only hurting person who existed, that everyone has a story. I had forgotten to open my eyes to those around me because I was so focused on my own problems. I was reminded that no one has it all together. I was reminded that more than ever the church, the bride of Christ, needs to lean on Jesus and each other to make it in this life. Also, the church needs to do a better job at seeking out the Nicoles all around, even if it's a Nicole who has been in church her entire life. There are always hurting people who need the hope of Jesus.

Got Your Six

When looking back at the story of Moses, Aaron, and Hur in Exodus 17, we see that Moses did not pretend that he was strong. He did not say to Aaron and Hur to back off, that he was strong enough to keep his arms up alone so that the battle could be won. He knew that the battle was God's, but he wanted to do his part to be faithful and worship during the battle in order to win. But when he became weak in his flesh and his arms began to shake, he did not stay prideful and pretend like he had it all together. In that moment, he was willing to accept help.

More importantly, Aaron and Hur had their eyes on Moses. Their eyes were open to the fact that Moses was getting tired. They were watching out for their brother in Christ and were able to step in right when he needed them the most. They were able to realize that he needed help, and they were willing to step in and provide him support. They were not too busy focusing on themselves and their backs were not turned from him. They were faithfully on close watch of Moses, and the battle was won.

We as a church need to be on close watch and make sure that we are doing all that we can to lift each other up. When the church operates in this way, the way that Jesus intended it to, then and only then will people outside the church walls want to be a part of the body of Christ and meet their Savior. Instead of being scattered, they will come together to worship the only One who can set them free.

A Beautiful Exchange

The truth is, Jesus will come back someday, and the body of Christ will be held accountable for how it has treated the world. Matt Chandler, one of my favorite speakers, men-

The truth is, Jesus will come back someday, and the body of Christ will be held accountable for how it has treated the world.

tioned in one of his sermons that the worst thing we can do about fear and anxiety is to pretend like they do not exist in us. I feel the same way about brokenness within the church. The worst thing that we can do as the bride of Christ is to pretend that we are all perfect, flawless, and do not have this constant need for the Savior.

When I personally began to realize that there was something truly beautiful about embracing my brokenness, even after I accepted Christ into my life, I felt freedom enter. I learned that the trick to life isn't to pretend like I have it all together. Life is about accepting who I am, where God has me, and constantly looking to Him to be the glue to hold my shattered life together. The truth is, we will always fall. We all have shortcomings. Paul even talked about the things he wanted to do but didn't do and the things he didn't want to do but did (Romans 7:15).

When we try to do things without Him, we fail. When we try to do things with Him, we still might fail, but He is with us to be our strength in our weakness. It is a beautiful exchange we have with the Son of the universe. When I accepted this reality, I was finally able to look beyond myself to those in the world around me. I wonder if the rest of the body of Christ is ready or willing to do the same?

Reflection:

Do you think that it is easier to build walls and keep others out or to build bridges and let others in? If it is easier for you to build walls up to keep others out are you ready to start letting Jesus break some walls down? Are you aware that the more people we let in, the more people we can help lift up?

Scripture Focus:

Romans 12: 10, "Show family affection to one another with brotherly love. Outdo one another in showing honor."

1 Corinthians 12: 25-26, "so that there would be no division in the body, but that the members would have the same concern for each other. So if one member suffers, all the members suffer with it; if one member is honored, all the members rejoice with it.

2 Corinthians 1: 3-7, "Praise the God and Father of our Lord Jesus Christ, the Father of mercies and the God of all comfort. He comforts us in all our affliction, so that we may be able to comfort those who are in any kind of affliction, through the comfort we ourselves receive from God. For as the sufferings of Christ overflow to us, so through Christ our comfort also overflows. If we are afflicted, it is for your comfort and salvation. If we are comforted, it is for your comfort, which is experienced in your endurance of the same sufferings that we suffer. And our hope for you is firm, because we know that as you share in the sufferings, so you will share in the comfort."

CHAPTER 20: THE TIME IS NOW

The church is a hospital for sinners,
not a museum for saints.

~Timothy Keller

We may impress people with our strengths.
But we connect with people through our weaknesses.

~Craig Groeschel
Dangerous Prayers

My husband's grandmother was a beautiful and amazing woman. She was shorter than all the rest of the family, but she stood tallest whenever she made the perfect grilled-cheese sandwich—seriously, it was the best I have ever tasted in my life…almost as good as my Nanny's chicken and dumplings. Also, her presence brought great comfort and peace in the midst of chaos. No matter what, she never raised her voice, but she knew how to keep the family in line with tactics such as a quick smack to a boy's shoulder. She was a wonderful God- fearing woman who always pointed the family back to the Lord.

Unfortunately for us but awesome for her, she got to see the glory of the Lord in 2013 when she left her earthly home. She is truly missed by all who knew her. Even though she is gone, I can still see visions of her in my mind, making her famous grilled-cheese sandwiches while talking about sunshine and JC. Aside from her amazing gift at the stove, and calming strategies, there was something else that she was phenomenal at, and I have yet to figure out how she obtained victory. She had a mysterious green thumb. She knew of all kinds of plants and understood exactly how to care for every single need of each plant in order to keep it alive.

My favorite place to be at her house was on the porch. The colors surrounding it were beautiful. When I walked up the stairs to reach my favorite destination, I would instantly feel better because of all the cheery colors all around. My favorite flower has always been the orchid, and from what I remember, she always had one going strong.

Every now and then, she would come to our house to visit. The first thing she usually did after she said hello was to find and point out the plant or flower that was about to die in our presence. Needless to say, I do not have a green thumb. In her gentle voice, she would take her time to explain to me all of the "how tos" in order to bring my plants back to life. I would do my best to listen intently and do exactly everything she prescribed. But even if I did precisely the things that she spoke of, the plant would still die in her absence.

I often fooled myself into thinking that if I did everything like Grandma and followed her rules of keeping plants alive, then my beautiful plants would stay alive. But the plants would quickly remind me

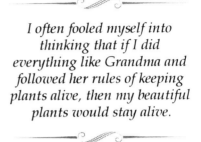

I often fooled myself into thinking that if I did everything like Grandma and followed her rules of keeping plants alive, then my beautiful plants would stay alive.

that I did not have all that it took. I had to accept over time that I would never get to live with a garden that looked like a picture from *Alice in Wonderland*. I did not have her gift of taking care of plants and knowing all that they needed to survive and thrive.

An Indescribable Love

God knew from the beginning of time exactly what the church would need in order to stay alive. The church didn't need another law to abide by or more Scripture to learn so it could be brighter than "those other Christians over there." The church definitely did not need a list of all the works that could be completed in order to tip the scales for God to show so-called favoritism with love, which isn't how God works at all. God knew that even if the church was given these things, each person within would fail greatly.

But God! He refused to leave the bride of Christ lost in her endless pursuit of perfection in things that would never satisfy. Instead of leaving her at the altar in her dirty white dress, caught in her distress and act of adultery with worldly and religious strides while simultaneously begging God for her groom, God chose to shed grace upon the church. He had mercy on her and desired to be close to her once again. He wanted to give her hope, setting her free from all her lies, deceit, and shortcomings. Compassionately, with all the love in His heart, He sent Jesus!

> But God! *He refused to leave the bride of Christ lost in her endless pursuit of perfection in things that would never satisfy.*

Jesus, the one and only groom, brings real freedom to His bride by giving her rest on every side. He longs for her to be safe in His arms without a care in the world. He doesn't think about her past or present falls; He wants only to love her, help her grow, and bring her a better future. He wants to be her provider. He desires to bring her rest. He proves to her over and over again that He wants to be her strength when she feels weak. He washes her as white as snow and leads her into everlasting life with Him.

Jesus brings real freedom for all, through Him. He, the Son of God, does not show favoritism like the church does. He desires for everyone to be in the bride of Christ, no matter the pit they come out of. He wants the adulterous woman to come to Him and weep at His feet. He wants the diseased that no one else wants to get near to come to Him and ask for a touch of His healing hands. He wants the child who is restless and demon possessed to run to Him for safety.

The Jesus who walked the earth wants every kind of person to come to Him, even if it means He is interrupted. Mark 2 describes a moment of chaos. Jesus was in the middle of speaking a message to so many people that there was no more room in the home they were meeting in. Concerned friends wanted to make their way to Jesus so that their paralyzed friend could be healed. The room was so crowded that

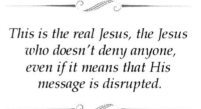

This is the real Jesus, the Jesus who doesn't deny anyone, even if it means that His message is disrupted.

they could not reach the Savior. They did the unthinkable task of cutting a hole in the roof and lowering their friend to Jesus. Jesus stopped what He is doing to heal the man, with friends full of faith, in front of Him. This is the real Jesus, the Jesus who doesn't deny anyone, even if it means that His message is disrupted.

Jesus even took it a step further and allowed a lifelong sinner to come to Him. In Luke 23, this amazing truth is revealed when He forgave a thief right before He uttered, "It is finished" before the Lord above and the world below. Christians who have walked their entire lives for the Lord might think, "Who is this man who got to go to heaven? He didn't live for the Lord. He didn't deserve salvation. That just isn't fair." But Jesus is a forgiver and welcomes anyone with a pure heart who longs to love Him and is desperate for Him. No matter how long it takes for them to realize His love for them, He pursues them even in their brokenness.

Only One Mediator

Now that being said, eventually there will be a time for the Judge to separate the sheep from the goats. The book of Matthew speaks of this truth in Matthew 25:31–46. In verses 32–34, Jesus declared: "Before him will be gathered all the nations, and he will separate people from one another as a shepherd separates the sheep from the goats. And he will place the sheep on his right, but the goats on the left. Then the King will say to those on his right, 'Come you who are blessed by my Father, inherit the kingdom prepared for you from the foundations of the world.'" One day all opportunity to come to Jesus will cease, the door will slam shut, and no one else will be able to enter the kingdom of heaven.

Does the bride of Christ continue to be the reason that some people will become goats banished to the left and separated for eternity from the Father in heaven? One day some will, and the church, individually and collectively, will be to blame. His grand design is for *all* to come to Him. First Timothy 2:3–4 says, "This is good, and pleasing in the sight of God our Savior, who desires all people to be saved and to come to the knowledge of the truth." This is the heart of the Father above. But has the church become a mediator between God and His desired children? In other words, has the church, like I did, tried to weed out people because they do not look, act, or dress like clones, believing they are too far-gone for us to help?

An old bluegrass hymn describes this truth all too well. There are various versions of this crazy hymn, but the frightening lyrics below of the song *Let the Church Roll On*, were performed by a band called Flatt and Scruggs at Carnegie Hall:

There's a deacon in the church (oh my Lord)
And he won't do right (oh my Lord)
What shall we do (oh my Lord)
Turn him out and kick him out
And let the church roll on

There's a drunkard in the church (oh my lord)
And he won't do right (oh my lord)
What shall we do, take the liquor pour it out,
And let the church roll on

There's women in the church (oh my lord)
Got paint on their face (oh my lord)
What shall we do take some water and wash it off,
And let the church roll on.

I am not sure if the lyrics shake anyone else, but to me, the words are extremely disturbing to the core. Believe it or not, the church does this daily. Unfortunately, I have done it. When I look back at the times I played Jesus or God and tried to weed out others because they didn't seem to belong in the church, it makes me sick to my stomach. In all honestly, it should make everyone in the church squirm a little bit because one day we will have to answer to the Father above.

Instead of looking at the deacon who has a problem and helping him, we kick him out. Instead of getting the drunkard help, we just dump the bottle out and pretend like the problem isn't there. As the body of Christ, we don't get him real help that is everlasting; we just brush off the issue. Instead of embracing the woman who wears too much makeup and getting to the bottom of why she does what she does, we just tell her to wash it off, shove the problem going on inside of her aside, and *let the church roll on.*

Truthfully, it is not the church's job to be the mediator between God and His people. Jesus is the one and only mediator. When reading further in 1 Timothy 2:5–6, we see that it very plainly declares, "For there is one God, and there is only one mediator between God and men, the man Christ Jesus, who gave himself as a ransom for all, which is the testimony given at the proper time." Jesus is the mediator, but somehow every singe individual has become a mediator, deciding who stays in the church, who gets weeded out, and who doesn't get invited at all in the first place.

The church's job is to be Jesus with skin on to everyone — not just the chosen few. We need to learn to accept people and their brokenness, just like Jesus does, because there is beauty in brokenness. There is beauty in the body coming together, loving Jesus, and locking arms with one another. There is beauty in saying, "Oh, come here, brother. You struggle with alcoholism? I struggle with so and so. Come and let us lean on each other! We are going to get through this together. More than that, we are going to give you the help you need, love you through the good and the bad, but more importantly, continue to point you to Jesus; the one who seeks out the broken to love them and set them free." The church's job is to say, "You are welcome here, a sinner who struggles daily, just like us."

His Church, His Bride

When others strive to break the arm-linked chain to become apart of the Family of God, the bride of Christ isn't to lock arms as tightly as we can to keep others out. We should not refuse to open our arms to welcome them in. We need to all realize that we do not have everything figured out and we will never have it together on our own. We need to open our arms to everyone because we *all* need Jesus. We *all* fall short. We are *all* a mess.

I had the hardest time accepting God's love because I thought I had to be perfect in order for Him to love me.

Additionally, I thought if I knew all the right scriptures, if I never thought bad things, if I sang the loudest, then Jesus and the church would finally accept who I was and keep me in the inner circle, their Family, to let me do ministry with them. I also thought for sure that Jesus Himself would finally love me. I have been in the church for over seventeen years of my life, but I have just now realized that I was living a lie. The world, too, needs to see the truth. The bride of Christ needs to extend a hand to point people to the grace that has been graciously given to *all* by the Father in heaven — Jesus.

The problem the church has today is trying to do things just like God without being God. Without Him, the church is nothing at all. Without Him, the church would cease to exist. But somehow we have conjured up in our minds the thought that we can do things like Him without Him. The church thinks that if it can just walk this tightrope of perfection, people will get saved. Church, we cannot save people. We cannot even save ourselves. We need Jesus more than the world needs mask-wearing Christians.

Church, we cannot save people. We cannot even save ourselves. We need Jesus more than the world needs mask-wearing Christians.

Jesus can do more in a second than the church can do in a lifetime. He is the Vine, and we are the branches. The church needs to remember to remain in Him because only He provides exactly what we need, exactly what everyone needs — His love. When we stay connected to the Vine, it isn't a sign of weakness; instead, it is a declaration that we are not superhuman but we are in touch with the only Superhuman in all of eternity. Jesus is the source of life for every part of this life and the next. Jesus is saying to the church, "I am the vine; you are the branches. The one who remains in Me and I in him produces much fruit, because you can do nothing without Me" (John 15:5). Church, we can do nothing without Him.

We may want big churches and tons of people to get saved, but by lifting up our picture-perfect lives, we are not doing anything at all for ourselves or anyone else. All we are doing is letting everyone down and stirring up frustration in the only one who truly matters in our lives, in our eternities — Jesus. If we embrace our brokenness and lift Him up, He will do the rest. John 12:32 reveals, "As for Me, if I am lifted up from the earth I will draw all people to Myself." *He* will draw people — not the flawless church service, pastor, worship session, skit, or building. None of those will do all that Jesus can do.

Jesus told Peter in Matthew 16:18, "And I also say to you that you are Peter, and on this rock *I will build My church*, and the forces of Hades will not overpower it" (emphasis added). I hope that the church gets this truth. *He* will build His church. We cannot build His church. When we try to do that oh so imperfectly, it will fall apart, people will get hurt, and we will anger our Father in heaven. When we do our job and point people to Jesus and lock arms with people, lifting them up in their struggles, Jesus will do His job and build His church by bringing salvation to all.

True Freedom

Freedom is in the midst of all these truths. When we finally accept that perfection isn't necessary, a burden is lifted off the shoulders of every Christian and every nonbeliever. On this side of eternity, we will all be broken in some way until Jesus calls each of us to be with Him. We no longer have to walk the tightrope of perfection. People on the outside do not have to try to wear the mask of religion in order to be like one of us on the inside, because we gladly accept that we are a mess and need Jesus to be the glue that constantly holds us together. Sheila Walsh an amazing woman of God who is a vocalist, songwriter, evangelist, author, and much more sheds light on this truth and declares, "My brokenness is a better bridge for people than my pretend wholeness ever was."

We need Him to survive. We need Him to thrive. Furthermore, the world needs Him to thrive. Without Him, it's falling apart.

Church, let's quit fooling ourselves, because we are not fooling anyone else around us. Let's be willing to embrace who we really are. We are broken. We need a Savior constantly, just like everyone else. We need Him to survive. We need Him to thrive. Furthermore, the world needs Him to thrive. Without Him, it's falling apart.

Let us step out of the way by being authentic, imperfect followers of Christ. He offers grace to all. He desires to love all. He desires to use us to be Jesus with skin on, to be children of light and to point people to the true light source. Church, we need to step down from the pedestal we have created for ourselves and constantly point everyone we can away from looking at us, and turn people to Jesus, the author and perfecter of all our faith.

Jesus is the only way. He is the one we are all looking for, and He is the one the rest of the world is looking for too. At the end of it all, when all else fades away, all that will be left is God, Jesus, their Words, the new heaven and earth, and all the saints who understood and believed these truths. We need to remove ourselves from the main focus and let true freedom come to the church as a whole and to the rest of the world. The time is now, church. The time is *now*!

Reflection:

1. *Have you been wearing a mask your whole life and tired of walking the tightrope of perfection?*
2. *Are you ready to wash your face and let your guard down completely and to let others know your shortcomings?*

3. *Are you ready to fully accept the fact that on this side of eternity that no matter how hard you try that you will never be perfect...that only Jesus can perfect us?*

4. *Are you ready to accept the unending grace and love of Jesus Christ and God in heaven?*

5. *Are you ready to accept the fact that you are not God and to step out of the way so that Jesus can use you to reach others in spite of your fallen human nature?*

A NOTE FROM THE AUTHOR:

If you answered 'yes' to all of these questions then you are ready for freedom and you better hold on because Jesus is going to do amazing things in your life and in the lives of those around you! If you have answered 'no' to these questions and you are not ready... just pray, give it some time, and allow these truths to sink deep into your heart. Jesus will do more in your life than you can ever imagine as you press into Him with a humble heart. Trust me...

Scripture Focus:

Psalm 51: 17, "The sacrifice pleasing to God is a broken spirit. God, You will not despise a broken and humble heart."

Artist: Disciple

Album: Scars Remain Released: 2006

Song: After the World

You break the glass, try to hide your face
Recorded lines that just will not erase
And buried in your loss of innocence
You wonder if you'll find it again

Was I there for the worst of all your pain?
And was I there when your blue skies ran away?
Was I there when the rains were flooding you off your feet?
Those were My tears falling down for you, falling down for you

I'm the One that you've been looking for
I'm the One that you've been waiting for
I've had My eyes on you ever since you were born
I will love you after the rain falls down
I will love you after the sun goes out
I'll have My eyes on you after the world is no more

Did I arrange the light of your first day?
Did I create the rhythm your heart makes?
Could you believe when your candle starts to fade?
I want to be the One that you believe
Could take it all away, take your heart away

253

Isn't My life a clear sign since I have crossed over this chasm
To fill the space between Me and you?
And I will do it all over again
Just look for Me, just wait for Me

The One you've been looking for
The One you've been waiting for
You won't have to look anymore

They conquered him by the blood of the Lamb and by the word of their testimony, for they did not love their lives in the face of death.

~Revelation 12:11

Running Mascara Study Guide

The following questions and scriptures are intended for deeper personal reflection or can be used to facilitate a seven-week small group discussion. If you choose to use this study as a group study then be sure to read the chapters assigned to the week you are on and read the questions in this guide prior to meeting with your group in order to be more prepared for each meeting. Part three and five are split into two weeks.

Week 1, Part 1: *Shattered* — Chapters 1-3

Chapter 1: My Happy Place

1. Were you able to think of a perfect moment or moments in your life?
2. Were you able to think about some bad things going on during those so-called "perfect" moments?
3. When realizing that the moments you thought of weren't perfect and still had flaws, did it ruin those moments for you?

4. Why do you think that we strive to have lives with out imperfections when even our perfect moments have flaws?

5. Do you agree with Psalm 34: 8; that no matter how much we strive to make the moments around us to be flawless in order to make us happy that only true happiness comes from God?

Chapter 2: The Dreaded Call

6. Where you able to recall a moment or moments in your life when everything seemed to fall apart?

7. Did these moments make you feel helpless?

8. Did the event or events change you as a person? If so where the changes good or bad?

9. Did you turn inward and become calloused to those around you or did you open up to others going through similar situations?

10. Did you feel as if the Lord walked with you through these events or did you feel like He was nowhere to be found and that you were completely alone? If you felt alone are you still angry with Him?

11. Have you healed completely from these tragedies or are you still holding on to them?

12. Are you ready to completely let go of them? If you answered 'no' then pray for God to soften your heart towards Him. Ask Him to help you hand

these tragedies over to Him, and pray that real healing comes.

Chapter 3: Mean Girls

13. Was it easy to recall a time or times in your life when people or groups of people ripped you apart as a person?

14. If it was easy to recall these events, how did it make you feel to go through these things?

15. Are you still holding onto those times and refusing to let go of the pain that they caused you?

16. Were you able to recall a time or times in your life when you were the person or apart of a group that tore someone else down?

17. Have you been holding on to the fact that someone hurt you or are you carrying the guilt of hurting someone else?

A NOTE FROM THE AUTHOR: *If you answered 'yes' to either of the situations in questions 17, in order for true healing and freedom to come in your life, it is vital to forgive. If you are able to get ahold of the person who hurt you, be honest with them about how it made you feel and tell them that you forgive them. If you were the one who hurt someone then contact him or her and ask for forgiveness. If it is impossible to contact these people then humbly seek the Lord with all of your heart and ask for forgiveness to come.*

READ OVER:

Matthew 6: 14-15, "For if you forgive people their wrongdoing, your heavenly Father will forgive you as well. But if you don't forgive people, your Father will not forgive your wrongdoing."

Matthew 18: 21-22, "Then Peter came up and said to him, "Lord, how often will my brother sin against me, and I forgive him? As many as seven times?" Jesus said to him, "I do not say to you seven times, but seventy-seven times."

DIVING DEEPER: How do these scriptures challenge you personally? How do these scriptures challenge you relationally with others and with God?

Week 2, Part 2: *A Glimmer of Hope* — **Chapters 4-6**

Chapter 4: My Lighthouse

1. In your life has there been a key person or persons who have drawn you to Jesus?
2. What type of qualities drew you to these people?
3. Were you able to find any flaws in these people?
4. If you were able to think of flaws in these people, does it open your eyes to the fact that God uses broken people in order to accomplish His will and draw people to Himself?

5. Are you aware that we are not called to be the light but draw others to the Light of life?

Chapter 5: The Early Church

6. Was there ever a time in your life when the church, the body of believers helped to fulfill your needs?
7. Is there a time that the church, the body of believers, failed to meet your needs?
8. Has there been a time in your life, when you helped fulfill someone else's needs?
9. Has there been a time in your life, when you failed to fulfill someone else's needs?
10. How can you improve on helping to fulfill others needs instead of always focusing on self?
11. Civil War Vet, Robert G. Ingersoll said, "We rise by lifting others." How do you think the church has failed to lift others up in this generation?
12. Do you think the church could do more if we became "one" as Jesus prayed instead of being so divided?

Chapter 6: Just a Carcass

13. Has anyone in your life gone out of his or her way to make you feel accepted?
14. How did it feel when they did this for you?

15. Have you ever gone out of your way to make a person or persons feel accepted? How did it feel?

16. Has their been a time when you have turned your face from someone who clearly needed acceptance?

A NOTE FROM THE AUTHOR: *People matter to God and they should matter to us. We need to put aside our pride and even if we look like total fools in the process…we need to reach out to those around us. Jesus constantly speaks light into our lives and we need to do the same for others by pointing others to Jesus…"the light of life." (John 8:12)*

READ OVER:

John 8: 12, "Then Jesus spoke to them again: "I am the light of the world. Anyone who follows me will never walk in darkness but will have the light of life."

John 17: 20-21, "I pray that not only for these, but also for those who believe in Me through their message. May they all be one, as You, Father, are in me and I am in You. May they also be one in Us, so the world may believe You sent me."

Hebrews 13: 2, "Don't neglect to show hospitality, for by doing this some have welcomed angles as gests with out knowing it."

DIVING DEEPER: How do these scriptures challenge you personally? How do these scriptures challenge you relationally with others and with God?

Week 3, Part 3A: *Masquerade* — Chapters 7-9

Chapter 7: Accidental Pharisee

1. What do you think about the quote by Elizabeth Christopher, "God simplifies. The devil complicates?"
2. Has their been a time in your life when you took striving for excellence a little too far? This can be in your every day life, in your relationship with Christ, or both.
3. Did you reach your goal of excellence?
4. If you did reach your goal did you feel better as a person or worse overall? If you didn't reach your goal did you feel like a complete failure?
5. Do you think that as the body of Christ, we focus too much on the stuff "to do" instead of pressing into our relationships with Jesus?

Chapter 8: Thin Cage

6. Can you think of a time in your life when you felt trapped in a situation and couldn't gain freedom?
7. What methods did you use in order to gain freedom?

8. Did you try to gain freedom on your own or did you press into Jesus for help?

9. If you still couldn't gain freedom, did it make you want to give up on everything; Maybe even to the point of wanting to take your own life?

Chapter 9: Wake-up Call

10. Was there a time in your life that God spoke clearly to you and you knew the exact next step you were to take but you didn't listen to Him?

11. Did you doubt that He was talking to you because you saw yourself too broken for a Holy God to speak to you?

12. Were you able to overcome the doubt and follow God in spite of yourself?

13. Is God speaking to you right now in your life to do something specific? Are you ready to say 'Yes Lord' and do it by pushing all doubt aside?

NOTE FROM THE AUTHOR: *There is no denying that we all face things in our lives that pull us away from a loving God. But are we aware that even godly things can draw us away from God? Does God want us to read His word? Of course! Does He want us to pray? Of course! Does he want us to worship Him? Of course! Does He want us to strive to be more like Jesus? Absolutely. But it's when our heart changes. When we turn from doing things* *out of the overflow of our love for Jesus to, "I have to do all of these things to be perfect, better than everyone else, and for God to love me," that is when danger steps in and we can get ourselves caught in a trap. Then we get to the point that we cannot even trust our relationship with God because everything about it is a façade. When He speaks to us it's impossible to hear Him because we have lost the ability to hear His voice clearly…we are distracted by so many other things. Today ask yourself, "Am I an accidental Pharisee? Am I trapped right now? Do I doubt everything about my relationship with God because I have grown so distant from Him by focusing on all of the wrong things?" If so, confess it to your group right now and seek healing. Ask your group to pray for you that you will not be tempted to fall back into old habits.*

READ OVER:

Look up Matthew 23: 1-36 and read it as a group.

John 8: 32, "You will know the truth, and the truth will set you free."

DIVING DEEPER: How do these scriptures challenge you personally? How do these scriptures challenge you relation-ally with others and with God?

Week 4, Part 3B: *Masquerade*—Chapters 10-12

Chapter 10: The Perfect Body

1. How did Caleb's story inspire you?

2. Do you know someone who is currently going through a similar situation, such as recent accident or a newfound disease that is keeping him or her to be limited? How are they handling it?

3. Have you personally gone or are going through a situation such as this? How are you handling it/dealing with it?

4. If you haven't gone through something like this before, do you think that you would maintain the spiritual integrity as Caleb has in his life? Would you be angry with God?

Chapter 11: The Heart of Jesus

5. Do you feel like you are a mess right now?

6. How does it make you feel to know that Jesus runs towards the messy?

7. Do you realize that pride keeps you in your mess?

8. Are you ready to let your walls down, embrace your mess today, and gain true freedom?

Chapter 12: I'm So Busy

9. Have you ever made your life busy on purpose in order to ignore a problem that you knew was there?

10. Have you made yourself busy in order to feel accomplished or feel of worth?

11. Today, are you like Martha or Mary?

12. If you are like Martha are you burnt out?

13. Have you heard the quote, "If the devil can't make you bad, he will make you busy," what do you think of it? Do you think it is true?

14. If you are like Mary, How can you share this great loving relationship with those around you?

A NOTE FROM THE AUTHOR: *The devil is jealous because he can never have what we have with the Father in Heaven. Since he is jealous, he tries to tell us that we have to be perfect before we run to Jesus. He does this to make us busy and worn out causing us to miss out on the real relationship with the Son of God that we have or could have. Even Christians who have been Christians for 20 plus years or more get caught in this pit time and time again. The truth is we do not need to be perfect before we come to Jesus. He welcomes all of the mess. Even before we committed our first sin, He loved us! We need to let Jesus tear down our walls, clean us up…again and again! Furthermore, let us not stay busy to ignore the real issues we have inside…the need for more of Jesus!*

When we are busy we think that we are doing something good but it leaves us empty. Let us sit at the feel of Jesus as Mary did to be filled up in every way and loved by Him…moreover, learn how we can reach others around us!

READ OVER:

1 John 4: 19, "We love because He first loved us."

Look up Luke 10: 38-42 and read as a group.

DIVING DEEPER: How do these scriptures challenge you personally? How do these scriptures challenge you relationally with others and with God?

Week 5, Part 4: *Running Mascara* — **Chapters 13-15**

Chapter 13: Behind Enemy Lines

1. Has fear ever gripped you to the point of paralyzing your way of life?
2. Are you aware that the devil uses fear to keep you from drawing closer to God and closer to others because he wants you to be alone?
3. Are you currently gripped by fear?
4. What types of fear are you ruled by today?

5. Are you aware that fear is a HUGE faith killer and can keep you from reaching your full potential in Christ?

Chapter 14: In the Desert

6. Have you ever had moments in your life where you felt like you were on a lonely island? When you were so desperate for God, His word, and fellowship with other people or believers but you were isolated?

7. Was the isolation that you were experiencing because of something beyond your control or was it caused by something you did?

8. Are you aware that most of the time we feel empty it is because we pull away, quit trying, and nothing else?

9. Do you feel lonely right now?

10. If you are lonely have you changed any of your habits that could have caused you to be in this position?

11. Are you aware that sometimes we have to work and fight for what we want? (See 2 Kings 3: 16-17)

12. What are some things that you can do in order to not feel so bone dry on a daily basis?

Chapter 15: Running Mascara

13. Have you ever been afraid to let others know that you weren't that strong and needed help?

14. Where you afraid of how others would see you by admitting you weren't perfect?

15. Today, do you feel like you have to be the "stronger sibling" or "super-Christian" in a situation?

16. Are you tired and worn out?

17. Are you ready to be weak so that Jesus can be your strength?

A NOTE FROM THE AUTHOR: *The devil is sneaky, very smart, and knows how to trap us. He is the father of lies according to John 8: 44. However, the problem isn't the fact that he is the father of lies, but that we start to believe his lies. Since we believe him, we start to push away from the Father, and distant ourselves from friends who can help us because we become too prideful to admit that we have issues. The devil makes us feel that if we let loose and tell the truth that no one will accept us so we do what he does best…we lie. Then when we think about how great we are or how much we have it "together" then we are blind to the fact that we need God in our lives constantly and fellowship with others to grow. Why do we let him fool us like this time and time again? If we were honest with ourselves and each other we would admit that none of us have our lives completely together. Even more than that…next to a Holy God, we are all shattered glass…disasters, but He choses to love us any way! God knows our weakness and our strengths but wants us to lean on Him in both! The truth is we don't have to be the "big brother or sister" any more! And by holding on to the idea of perfection we are only hurting ourselves!*

LET IT GO brothers and sisters in Christ! LET IT GO! We need God in our lives. We need each other in our lives! We know we cannot do life alone!

*If you have tried to carry a burden or burdens by yourself in fear of what others would think confess it before the Lord and others in your group. Pray for each other that all of you would lean on God for help and each other more than ever.

READ OVER:

2 Kings 3: 16-17, "Then he said, "This is what the Lord says: 'Dig ditch after ditch in this wadi.' For the Lord says, 'You will not see wind or rain, but the wadi will be filled with water, and you will drink – you and your cattle and your animals."

Psalm 16: 2, "I said to Yahweh, "You are my Lord; I have nothing good besides You."

Proverbs 27: 16, "Iron sharpens iron, and one man sharpens another."

2 Corinthians 12: 9, "But He said to me, 'My grace is sufficient for you, for your power is perfect in weakness.' Therefore I will most gladly boast all the more about my weaknesses, so that Christ's power may reside in me."'

1 John 4: 18, *"There is no fear in love; instead, perfect love drives out fear, because fear involves punishment. So the one who fears has not reached perfection in love."*

DIVING DEEPER: How do these scriptures challenge you personally? How do these scriptures challenge you relationally with others and with God?

Week 6, Part 5A: *White Flags* — Chapters 16-18

Chapter 16: Surrender

1. Have you completely surrendered everything in your life to Jesus — all of your best and all of your worst?
2. What parts of your life have you refused to lay down to Him and wave your "white flag" of surrender?
3. Do you realize that you are nothing with out Him and by acting like you have it all together is only hurting yourself?
4. If you have surrendered everything to Him, are you ever tempted to pick things back up?
5. Is there something currently that you have picked back up? If so then ask your group to pray for you, that you have the strength to lay it down and never pick it back up again.

Chapter 17: Starving the Body

6. Have you pursued religion instead of Jesus any time in your life?
7. If you have perused religion instead of relationship with Jesus did you feel full or empty during your pursuit?
8. Do you think that as Christians we are being good examples of what a relationship with Jesus really looks like?
9. Do you think non-believers see us as miserable followers of Christ?
10. Would Jesus be happy with us as individual followers of Christ and collectively as the church today?
11. Are we driving people away form the church because they will never rise to the occasion because of the perfect masks we wear and the measuring sticks we have created?
12. Are we trying to build up the numbers of our church by putting on a show in order to feed our own egos instead of offering more of Jesus?

Chapter 18: What Church?

13. Have you ever been asked to leave a church because you did not act, look, or talk like everyone else in the church?

a. If you answered 'yes' how did it make you feel?

b. Did it take you a long time to step back into a church?

c. Are you still running from church today because of the events that took place?

d. Did the situation destroy the relationship you had with God or Jesus, or did it keep you from wanting a relationship with them at all?

14. Have you ever asked someone to leave a church because they did not act, look, or talk like everyone else?

a. Did you feel like you were "helping God out" by asking them to leave?

b. Did you feel good about yourself when you did it, like God should be patting you on the back because you got the "sinner" out? Or are you angry with yourself for acting the way that you did?

c. Are you aware that you can ask God for forgiveness in these areas and ask for another chance to extend mercy to someone else like He has to you?

15. How do you think God feels about both situations in questions 13 and 14?

a. Do you think that He values you over another person?

b. Do you think that He detests both situations?

c. Do you realize that other people are just as important as you are and that you are just as important to Him as other people?

A NOTE FROM THE AUTHOR: *In his book 'Crazy Love' Francis Chan reveals, "We need to stop giving people excuses not to believe in God. You've probably heard the expression 'I believe in God, just not organized religion'. I don't think people would say that if the church truly lived like we are called to live." Do you feel as if the church is acting the way that we should towards others? Are we extending the type of grace and mercy that God extends to us on a second by second basis? If we would remain in a continuous state of surrender to God then we would realize how much we really need Him. We would realize that with out Him we would starve in every area of our lives. With this type of attitude humility would draw us on our knees before a Holy God…realizing we are nothing with out Him. We would be reminded that we were once in the situation that the unbeliever finds himself or herself… lost and in desperate need for a Savior… for hope. We would have no need to ask people to leave the church because they are a little different. Am I saying to not face and deal with sin? Absolutely not! But to pretend that we do not sin, that we do not need God, and that "that person over there needs Him more than I do," is just insanity. We all fall short, we all need Him, and we would be fools to think any less.*

READ OVER:

Job 1: 20-21, "Then Job stood up, tore his robe, and shaved his head. He fell to the ground and worshiped, saying: Naked I came from my mother's womb, and naked I will leave this life. The Lord gives, and the Lord takes away. Praise the name of Yahweh."

Romans 3: 9, "What then? Are we any better? Not at all! For we have previously charged that both Jews and Gentiles are all under sin, as it is written: There is no one righteous, not even one."

Look up John 8: 1-11, and read as a group.

DIVING DEEPER: How do these scriptures challenge you personally? How do these scriptures challenge you relationally with others and with God?

Week 7, Part 5B: *White Flags* — **Chapters 19-20**

Chapter 19: Freedom

1. Why do you think that we build walls instead of bridges to other people as Jesus does?
2. Have you been so focused on self that you have failed to notice the "Nicole's" around you?
3. How does the account of Moses, Aaron, and Hur, inspire you, challenge you, or both?

4. Do you think that the church, individually and collectively, have put blinders on to those who are really struggling inside and outside the church?

5. Do you think the church has an, 'us' verses 'them' mentality?

6. Do you think that if Jesus came back today, He would be happy with the way the church has cared for His Bride or possible people that could be apart of His Bride?

7. Are you ready to break free...completely free from the walls you have built up...so that Jesus can do what He wants in your life and in the lives of those around you?

Chapter 20: The Time is Now!

8. Have you been wearing a mask your whole life and tired of walking the tightrope of perfection?

9. Are you ready to wash your face and let your guard down completely and to let others know your shortcomings?

10. Are you ready to fully accept the fact that on this side of eternity that no matter how hard you try, that you will never be perfect...that only Jesus can perfect us?

11. Are you ready to accept the unending grace and love of Jesus Christ and God in heaven?

12. Are you ready to accept the fact that you are not God and to step out of the way so that Jesus can use you to reach others in spite of your fallen human nature?

A NOTE FROM THE AUTHOR: *When we pretend like we have it all together it's like looking in a mirror and telling ourselves that our skin is flawless, only to turn on a black light and see the truth for all that it really is…that our skin is covered in sunspots and all kinds of imperfections. Next to a Holy God, we are all full of sin, blemishes, and shortcomings. We need to quit trying to fool ourselves in thinking that we have it all together because we do not. We need Jesus, the one and only Savior of this world to cleanse us from all unrighteousness and all impurities. We also need to realize that His washing is a life long process. We often think that when we are saved that is it…we are whole and we do not need Jesus any more. Is our salvation secure? Absolutely! But does that mean that we do not need Him constantly? Absolutely not! The sanctification process is a life long process. He is here to constantly wash us of the grit that tries to attach itself to us in this world, before we step into His pure kingdom. We need Him church and there is a world out there that needs Him too! We need to accept His washing constantly, let our walls down, and do what He sent us here to do in the first place. He did not create us to build our own lives up and forget Him and others. He sent us here to do a mission…to draw people to Him by being the hands and feet of Jesus. Join me in reaching out to people and showing them the LOVE that never fails! Let us remain humbled and broken before* the God of the universe! Only He can make us whole! Only He can make the world whole! We need to step aside Church, step aside! The time is NOW!

READ OVER:

Psalm 51: 17, "The sacrifice pleasing to God is a broken spirit. God, You will not despise a broken and humble heart."

Romans 8: 38-39, "For I am persuaded that not even death or life, angels or rulers, things present or things to come, hostile powers, height or depth, or any other created thing will have the power to separate us from the love of God that is in Christ Jesus our Lord!"

1 John 1: 9, "If we confess our sins, He is faithful and righteous to forgive us our sins and to cleanse us from all unrighteousness."

Look up Colossians 1: 15-23, and read as a group.

DIVING DEEPER: How do these scriptures challenge you personally? How do these scriptures challenge you relationally with others and with God? How do these scriptures bring freedom to you? How can these scriptures bring freedom to those around you?

About the Author

Tiffany Wasson has been in ministry in some form or fashion since she was 14 years old. Her journey started out at Lighthouse Christian Broadcasting in Saint Marys, Georgia, as a youth leader, on air minister, and radio show host. Currently, she resides in Augusta, Georgia, with her husband, two kids, and two dogs. In her daily life she likes to write, run, and laugh as much as possible. Overall she is passionate about helping the church in any way that she can, especially youth groups. She longs to see the next generation constantly looking to Jesus, the author and perfector of their faith (Hebrews 12:2).

CPSIA information can be obtained at www.ICGtesting.com
Printed in the USA
LVOW11s0503190316

479831LV00002B/3/P